WISE GUYS FINISH FIRST

LEARNING MY WAY TO THE TOP

WISE GUYS FINISH FIRST

LEARNING MY WAY TO THE TOP

BY

SOLOMON
HICKS

WITH MICHELLE JONES

First Edition

Printed in the United States of America

Cover design by Esther Han
Inside text layout and design by Page Design of Los Angeles, CA

ISBN-13: 978-0-9789346-0-6
ISBN-10: 0-9789346-0-1

Contents

INTRODUCTION: *This Little Light of Mine*   9

1. *Entertaining Angels*   17

2. *Winner By Design*   41

3. *At First Sight*   55

4. *Labor Pains*   71

5. *Choice*   85

6. *Counting The Cost*   101

7. *In The Dark*   115

8. *Let It Shine*   141

9. *Now It's Personal*   153

INTRODUCTION

This Little Light of Mine

Then I saw that wisdom excels folly as light excels darkness.
                    —SOLOMON (Ecclesiastes 2:13)

If you have knowledge, let others light their candles in it.
                    —MARGARET FULLER

The goal…is not for you to know my story, but to use my story in order to uncover your own.

                    —SOL HICKS

ॐ ॐ

You do not have this book in your hands by accident.

I don't know if you bought it or received it as a gift. You could have found it, borrowed it, or even stolen it. For all I know you could have grabbed it to balance out the legs of an uneven table or because you needed a coaster for that hot mug of coffee in your hands. How you got this book is not really the point anymore than it matters what Da Vinci's cat had for breakfast the day he finished the Mona Lisa. Why you have it is what matters. Why you? Why now? Why here, at this specific juncture of your life, possessing your particular history of moments concerning you?

I have been asking "why?" from time to time as this

work comes together. You see, writing a book was not originally my idea. It was my mother's. "Tell your story," she said to me years ago. "You will help a lot of people who think they can't be anyone." Before that day, I didn't know I had a story to tell. Then with that one expressed thought, mom made visible the harvest of what God had planted in me through her.

When I was born, she decided that my name would be Solomon after the boy king in the Bible who would become the wisest man who ever lived. She wanted me to love wisdom. My nickname would be Sol, Spanish for "sun," because she prayed that I would be a light for others. That was no small prayer where we lived.

I grew up in the very small, very southern town of Eufaula, Alabama, at a time when Segregation was still alive and thriving in America. Young black boys weren't expected to become much besides old black men. When they took the time to discuss our futures, our teachers— some sincerely believing they were being constructive— discouraged any ambition we had beyond becoming farmers. Now, while that was—and still is—respectable work, it was not the work I was fashioned for or called to.

Recently I retired from Prudential Insurance where I spent 35 years as an agent. I am arguably the most successful agent in the history of that and possibly any insurance organization. I have an unbelievable wife who still tells me I'm handsome, talented and wonderful after 42 years of marriage. My children and grandchildren have never given me a moment without joy, not one. I have been privileged to travel and share my experiences with agents, agencies, churches, and businesses all over the world. Even in my first years of retirement, I still mentored a few dozen insurance agents. More than 80% of them qualified for the

Million Dollar Round Table, most of them for the first time in their careers.

These are grand statements, I know, and I don't make them to be grand or as hyperbole, but to make one point: This life—my life—is, in the words of the apostle Paul, "exceeding abundantly above all that I could ever ask or even think," but it is not the life I set out to live. Rather, it is the life that was God's gift to me before He placed me in my mother's womb. It is the life He sent me into this world to live, and the one He has committed Himself to empowering me to live through His Holy Spirit. It is the life He promised my mother when she gave me my name. It is the only life that answers every deep desire of my heart.

- Are you living the life that daily answers the deepest desires of your heart? Do you know what those desires are?

- Is your life bigger than your own imagination and greater than people's expectations?

- Do you know what you were sent here to say to the world through your particular set of circumstances? Do you have the courage to devote your life to saying it, no matter what it costs you?

- Can you see the tools that God has placed at your feet to help you discover every promise He made to you before He breathed life into you?

- Are you ready to live exceeding abundantly beyond all that you could ask or even think?

These questions are the reason you have this book in your hand. Helping you answer "yes" to all of them is the reason it was written.

Tell Your Story...

Sometime after telling me I should write a book, my mother had an appointment with a doctor who informed her that she was very ill. I remember the day she called to tell me about it. As she talked, I guess I imagined what most people would, a sober and serious man in a white coat sitting in a large chair behind a larger desk. The thought of my mother having to bear the weight of any painful news without my shoulder to lean on was almost too much to take. My heart was breaking for her, and for myself, when she said he told her that her cancer was beyond curing and that she had just three to six months to live. *Three to six months?* I didn't know what to say. Mom did though. She didn't blink. She said she told the doctor, "I sure am glad your name ain't Jesus!" When she told me that, I had to laugh.

As these words travel down to take their place on this page, other words make their way up from me to find the ears of God. He inclines daily to hear my prayers for my mother who is fighting to keep weight on her frail 98-pound frame. She is tired and hurting. It's November right now. Thanksgiving is just a few days away and she says she may not be able to join us for dinner. I don't know if she will make it with me to the end of the writing of this book. It is worth mentioning however that it has been three years—that's right, years, not months—since her conversation with the serious and sober doctor whose name clearly wasn't Jesus.

I have been thinking a lot lately about the shortness of life and how urgently we have to love one another. As I serve my mother in whatever way I can, I learn more and more about the relationship between "being" and "becoming." As I cook for her, run errands for her, listen to her, hold her, wipe her tears, or just make her laugh, I see that I am only doing for her what she has always done for me.

Love given plants a seed that one day produces a desire to serve the way we have been served, to comfort in the manner that we have been comforted, to forgive the way we have been forgiven, and to extend mercy and grace as we have received them.

I want to tell you my story. It's not a poor-kid-becomes-a-rich-man story. Nor is it a boy-gets-girl, hard-work-pays-off, weakness-overcomes-strength, restoration-after-setback, perseverance, forgiveness, amazing-grace, or finding-your-destiny story. All of those stories are contained in my story, but they are not the focus of it.

Mine is a story about two things: loving wisdom and being light. This is the sum and substance of my inheritance, my legacy, and my learning. It is all I have to give or will ever have. And as I tell my story, I hope you will see that it is not just a gift from me to you, but a gift of me to you.

How to Use This Book

This book is autobiographical. However, I will tell you again and again that it is not about me. The goal as you read it is not for you to know my story, but to use my story in order to uncover your own.

I want to do for you what my mother and others I'll mention later have done and continue to do for me. I want to inspire you. My hope is that you will find encouragement in these pages. I have already prayed that you would be challenged; that you would be willing to see everything in your heart, even the dark things. I expect God to use this book to call out what He has already put in you and root out what He hasn't. I hope you make up your mind to fight when you have to, lay down when you're told to, and let go when you're asked to. And if you're struggling at this particular point in your life with anything, I hope that as you read you will know that you're not alone.

There are nine short chapters following. You should be able to read this book in one sitting, but I hope you don't. Spend as much time as you need to on each chapter, even if it takes days. You're not reading so much as *searching*. Take your time. Think, meditate, listen, and pray. Finishing the book won't matter if you're not allowing the Holy Spirit to work on finishing you.

At the end of each chapter, you will be given some space designed to give you an honest look at the condition of your life. You will be asked to write down some things in the space provided. Don't skip this part. You will look back at what you wrote on these pages one day and I promise you'll have reasons to praise God.

You will also be challenged to make some decisions, choices, or changes in light of what you've learned. Write those down as well, even if you're afraid you won't stick to them or if you've tried and failed at the same thing time and again. It may discourage you to be reminded of falling, but a blank page means you're not trying to push yourself past your limits, or you're failing and trying to hide. Neither of those behaviors will help you grow.

Finally, at the very end, you will be asked to take some time to meet with a friend and share what you have experienced and learned. Ask them to keep you accountable for what you have written and what God has shown you or said to you. Have that person pray with you, for you, and then about you during his/her personal prayer time. Nothing good is accomplished by God's people apart from God's people. Connection, communion, and community are vital to your successes, and they become even more valuable to you when you suffer defeats or setbacks.

You may even try going through the entire book with a friend. As the pair of you spends time together, discussing each chapter, you can push and challenge one another to reach for new levels of self-discovery, prayer, confession, obedience, courage, faith, love, and humility. Solomon (the king, not I) said, "two are better than one, because they have a good reward for their labor [and] if they fall, the one will lift up his fellow, but woe to him that is alone when he falleth; for he hath not another to help him up." (Eccl. 4:9, 10)

Matthew 5:16 exhorts us to "let your light so shine before men, that they may see your good works, and glorify your Father which is in heaven." Think about that for a minute. Your life should "shine" or be visible to people in such a way that as they believe what they see in you, they become more like the God you've been serving. We don't glorify someone simply by saying good things about them. That's praise. Glory happens when we manifest and reflect who they are. Glory goes beyond imitation to transformation. If that seems like an awesome responsibility God has placed on our shoulders, then you're already one step closer to getting it. You are your brother's keeper, and he is yours.

I am your brother, and I want to be a good steward of your attention. My prayer for you, from introduction to end, is that you would be transformed into a man or woman anxious to tell the world the story you were sent here to tell. In other words, my story will be told most brilliantly when and if you are shining most brilliantly.

CHAPTER ONE

Entertaining Angels

I [Wisdom] love those who love me, and those who seek me diligently will find me.
—SOLOMON (PROVERBS 8:17)

I am somehow less interested in the weight and convolutions of Einstein's brain than in the near certainty that people of equal talent have lived and died in cotton fields and sweatshops.
—STEPHEN JAY GOULD

As a young boy, I was always searching for wisdom…Now that I'm older, I realize that wisdom has always been searching for me; waiting on my curiosity and looking for every opportunity to put wise people in my path.
—SOL HICKS

ॐ ॐ

I had my first real job at 9 years old. Every weekend I washed dishes, pumped gas, and waited on drive-up customers at the Drive 'Round It, a 24-hour restaurant/

truck stop in Eufaula, Alabama. I earned $2/night, all of which I gave to my mother, brother, and sisters. I worked Fridays, Saturdays, and Sundays from 9pm 'til 6am, which meant that on Monday mornings I would come home from work, take a nap, change clothes, and then head right back out to my "non-paying gig"—the fourth grade.

Sometimes it was tough. Sometimes I couldn't take my Monday-morning nap if I had homework due. I didn't play marbles or baseball. There wasn't time for such things even if I had wanted to indulge. I think back on my childhood often. It's only natural that maturity has clarified some things for me and given shape and reason to others. I see life through a man's eyes and not those of a little boy. Despite that, my now sixty-something mind and that 9-year-old one continue to agree on one thing: Those were some of the best times of my life.

I don't have any enduring memories of school, good or bad. Most people can recall a favorite teacher, a class clown, a special crush, even an embarrassing moment or a not-so-pleasant experience with a bully. Not me. School was not overly fun, or traumatic, or angst-filled. It was just school. It was the place I went to when I wasn't working. Work, on the other hand, was what transformed me; not so much the work itself, but the experiences which came through the work.

I remember begging my mother to let me get a job. She didn't want me to, but I was determined to have my way. She and my father divorced when I was 3, and even though she had remarried my stepfather who was a good, hard-working man, I still felt responsible for her and my brother and sisters. I daydreamed about being able to provide for them and be a source of strength and support for them.

It never occurred to me that "normal" 9-year-olds had

much sillier things on their minds. I didn't know that I should be running from girls, eating everything in sight, racing go-carts and bicycles, wearing holes in my jeans, or attaching myself to every dirty or muddy thing I could find. I was an odd child. I got the most joy out of the conversation of older people. I would sit by my aunts and listen to them talk. I helped my mother and grandmother in the kitchen and they taught me how to cook.

There was something about people with wrinkled skin or gray hair that made me want to hear and value what they had to say. They just looked like they knew more than other people, so whenever I encountered them, I asked every question that came into my head, and these amazing, wonderful women and men shared their knowledge and experiences with me. They confirmed, time and again, what I often suspected: there is always something more to learn.

I was more than just curious. Curiosity is satisfied with the mere accumulation of information. I wanted more than that. I wanted to know how to use information in a way that would make me as successful as the people I admired. I didn't measure success in terms of money or possessions. I still don't. Not that I have a problem with people who do. That's just never been my way. I couldn't have put into words what made one man successful and another not when I was a boy. I just had an inner confidence about certain people, a sort of "knowing in my knower" that they were living right, and I wanted to live right too, so I pursued them.

Many years later, I can tell you what all the people I have ever called successful have in common; what they poured out that I was always thirsty for. They were WISE. They didn't just have knowledge, and they did more than just use the information available to them. They used their knowledge as a tool for personal growth that would lead to making good decisions. Good decisions are those decisions which give you the freedom to be good and to do good for others. That is how I define wisdom, and it's what I believe was at the heart of my mother's prayers for me when she named me Solomon.

> **WISDOM is the willingness to make the choices that give you the freedom to be good and to do good for others.**

Every successful person is wise in some way. I believed that as a child, and I believe it now. Some are wise with money. Others are wise in relationships. Bill Gates is a wise businessman. Bono is a wise communicator, Mother Theresa a wise advocate. My mother is a wise teacher, my wife is wise counsel to me and others, and my daughters are wise parents to their children. I work with ministers who are wise shepherds and I have encountered many wise leaders, managers, and servants behind the scenes.

Dr. Martin Luther King Jr. was a wise influencer of people, C.S. Lewis a wise igniter of imaginations. Van Gogh, Rembrandt, and Michelangelo revealed their wisdom in their art. Abraham was a wise father, and John the Baptist was a wise steward of the gospel until it arrived in the person of his cousin Jesus Christ.

True wisdom is not something we're born with, but rather something that is available to us and for us from the day we're born. A "wise" toddler fears a spanking and makes the choice to leave the cookies in the cookie jar until she is offered one. A wise teenager chooses to study *before* the test. A wise twenty-something decides to leave the nightclub early if he has to work tomorrow. A wise husband doesn't live above his means, has only as many children as he can love and support, manages time efficiently, and plans for retirement.

Wisdom is a gift from God, but make no mistake; it is not some mystical, invisible vapor of intuition or a miraculous cranial impartation that puts a man or woman above "mere mortal" thinkers. When we envision wise people, we often imagine individuals with intellectual or philosophical fortitude who offer solutions and resolutions for life's conundrums. In actuality, real wisdom has very little to do with how we think about life. More accurately it is the willingness to *do* life well.

Etymologically, the word "wise" comes from a root that means "to see" but wisdom is more than simply seeing the right way. It is going that way. In fact, wisdom that isn't practiced is not wisdom. Think about it. I can *see* that my blood pressure is high and that I am at risk for a heart attack, but does seeing that mean I'm wise, or does wisdom kick in when I take action to change my diet and set out to eliminate the stress in my life?

Wisdom is as mundane as paying the phone bill and as practical as a good night's sleep. Like food, it only helps us grow if we digest it and let it nourish our behavior. Then as we grow, so too does our capacity to receive and pursue more of it. Wisdom only increases in us to the degree that we live out what wisdom has already shown us. Jazz great Charlie Parker said it best: "If you don't live it, it won't come out of your horn."

As a young boy, I was always searching for wisdom, though I wouldn't have called it that. I only knew that there were people around me who didn't struggle to be nice, could forgive easily, enjoyed learning, weren't afraid of what they didn't know, shared what they did know, worked hard and still smiled, endured pain without complaining, had joy and hope, and told the truth even when it could bring them harm.

I thought these people were heroes. I was convinced that they could do anything they could imagine, and I couldn't imagine anything more wonderful than having that kind of freedom. So I chased them…*until they caught me!*

You didn't misread that. If I put myself in the mind of young Sol, I was the pursuer, anxious to learn all that these people had to teach me. All of my questions—and there were many of them—were met with equal parts of patience and generosity that I didn't immediately see. I only knew that these were seemingly bottomless wells of everything I wanted to know, so I drank…and drank…and drank.

When we're young, we focus on our own thirst and see people in terms of their ability to sate us. However, with time, our emotional palate becomes more dignified, and we find ourselves more interested in the experience of our encounters. We begin to give real attention to the well we have been visiting. We are curious to know now how it was dug, or we notice the plants which grow around it. We wonder about the shape of it; how deep it goes, or how much rain needs to fall in order to fill it.

Then something very special happens. In the maturing of relationship, when our need is less desperate and consumption has surrendered to companionship, the other half of "us" becomes truly visible. We aren't as conscious anymore of our own greedily cupped hands or our own open throat gulping and swallowing. From this newly broadened perspective, instead of only seeing ourselves taking, we begin to understand that we are also being *given to*. What appears to our wizened eyes is the joy of the one giving himself or herself to us and we realize that what we thought was a well, is in actuality a spring bubbling up before us.

A well waits to be approached and allows itself to be used without really participating in the event. Springs offer their water up because they can't help it. They're not made for water, but formed by it. Wells hold water. Springs release it.

I have read and been told the story of Solomon my whole life. I know that he asked for wisdom to rule a kingdom he inherited as a boy.

> That night the LORD appeared to Solomon in a dream, and God said, "What do you want? Ask, and I will give it to you!"
>
> Solomon replied, "…O LORD my God, you have made me king… but I am like a little child who doesn't know his way around…Give me an understanding mind so that I can govern your people well and know the difference between right and wrong…" The Lord was pleased with Solomon's reply and was glad that he had asked for wisdom. So God replied, "Because you have asked for wisdom in governing my people and have not asked for a long life or riches for yourself or the death of your enemies—I will give you what you asked for! I will give you a wise and understanding mind such as no one else has ever had or ever will have! And I will also give you what you did not ask for--riches and honor! No other king in all the world will be compared to you for the rest of your life!" (1 Kings 3:5-13)

The boy in me wanted wisdom, and received it wherever I found it. Then, as I grew, I began to see my quest for wisdom with new eyes. It's easy to look at the story of King Solomon in terms of that boy's need, but look at it again, and this time focus your attention on the behavior of God. He instigated that conversation with Solomon. He directed it, and decided the outcome of it. When you look at Solomon's life from the standpoint of God's actions, what becomes obvious is this: Solomon didn't initiate his search for wisdom. God did. God was eager to teach, so He made Solomon eager to learn.

God never left His teaching job. Like that young king, I was "awakened" in my circumstances. My father wasn't around; we had little money and a lot of mouths to feed. I don't really remember when or where the idea came to me, but my 9-year-old mind had somehow latched onto the conclusion that I could, and should take on the responsibility of caring for my family. I knew that it was something I wanted very badly, but I also knew that it wouldn't happen simply because I wished it, so I looked for people to imitate and learn from.

The bible says that all true wisdom comes from God, and that He'll give it liberally to anyone who asks for it. In other words, wisdom was around long before I was, and wisdom has always been searching for me; waiting on my interest and looking for every opportunity to put wise people in my path. God has been that aforementioned water anxious to satisfy me, drawn to the surface of kind and caring people by my thirst, my desire to be good and do good for others, and released by their willingness to give what He had given to them during their lives.

I originally thought they were heroes. More accurately they were angels, divine messengers some, protectors others. They encouraged me, taught me, nurtured me, directed me, corrected me, and lit a path for me as I entertained them. They exposed me to a world beyond Eufaula Alabama and pushed me to reach for it. They cheered me on in my dreaming and gave me the gift of their faith in me when mine wasn't enough. I think the wonder of these beautiful people was not so much in what they said to me as in how they lived what they said. Remember, wisdom is not how you think but what you do. They showed me what it looked like to do life well.

I'm beginning this book about my life talking to you about people other than me because without them, I would have very little to say. If this book were simply the story of the events of my life, I doubt that I would have made any effort to produce it. There are plenty of lives more eventful than mine. I have no great desire to show you how to be me or how to accumulate what I have. I think God has too much imagination to want to see the same life lived over and over. However, we all have a particular contribution to make. Each of us, by our living, uniquely informs and educates another for better or worse.

One of the great values of human life is found in its ability to influence other human life. Knowing that we can be influenced gives us reassurance that we can be more than we are. Knowing that we can influence others gives us a reason to be more than we are. I am fortunate to have been shaped by many generous and exceptional people. They are integral to any telling of my story, and because of what they poured into me, I have a life worth pouring out for others. I will share briefly about three of them.

My mother, **Rosie L. Stanford**, is one of the strongest women I know. Even now with cancer keeping her in constant pain and physically weak, she looks at me and I still see the person she has always been, full of faith, determined, certain of what she knows, gracious, and willing to give her last to anyone in need.

I learned how to give from my mother. As I said before, we didn't have much, but she never let it settle into us that we were "have nots." Everyone was always welcome at our house. When people came over, the first thing mom would do is go in the kitchen and cook. (That gift of hospitality has made its way to me. If you visit me at my home in Atlanta, expect to eat.) She could magically make whatever food we had stretch to feed us and whoever else was there.

Mom was tolerant before Tolerance became a worthy ideal in America. She wouldn't allow us to be militant even though we could have thought of many reasons to be that way in segregated Eufaula, Alabama. I never heard her talk negatively despite the challenges she and others faced. When I asked her about it, she'd only say that we were all God's children and I took that to mean that getting bitter was not an option.

I decided to focus on caring for my family. I was excited about working and sharing the $2.00 I earned each night with them. It wasn't a lot, but I never knew it. My mother received it from me as a genuine contribution to our household. She encouraged my desire to provide. She could have diminished my efforts by saving what I gave her and giving it back to me when I was older, or she could have just told me to keep it. But she was wise enough to know that she was planting something valuable in me, something that would prepare me for a family of my own.

One night I went to work and was told that our cook hadn't shown up. Right away I volunteered, first because I loved to cook. Second, because a cook at the Drive 'Round It earned $3.00 a night! I had been waiting for the opportunity to be considered for that job. Thomas Edison once said, "Opportunity is missed by most because it is dressed in overalls and looks like work." I was determined not to miss this. I knew that I was going to have one chance to prove I could be twice as good as anyone they could think of hiring.

I flipped, grilled, fried, chopped, mashed, baked, and mixed with everything I had in me. My hands were fast and my smile was big. More important, the food was G-O-O-D good! I pulled out every delicious trick I had learned from my mother. Thanks to her, I went home the next morning with a new job.

Solita Hortman paid a visit to the restaurant after I had been cooking there for awhile. She was new to Eufaula, a businesswoman with plans to open a restaurant in town. She wanted to see how a successful establishment was run and perhaps get an idea or two. However, she was not prepared for what would happen during her visit, neither of us was. It would change both our lives forever.

She took her place at the counter and ordered her meal. I saw her from the kitchen as I was working and greeted her with my best smile. She returned the greeting, and watched me cook until her meal came. I remember she seemed pleased with it, stayed awhile, and then left. She returned a few more times after that.

Then one day she came in and I was surprised to learn that she wanted to talk to me. We chatted about nothing particularly important, my age, my family, school, and work. "How much money do you make here?" she wanted to know. I told her, and after a moment she said, "I'll pay you $20.00 a week to come work for me." That was more money than I could imagine at the time. I thought I must have really done my thing in that kitchen the other day! The truth is Miss Solita did like my cooking, but I would learn later that I had her attention well before that.

Miss Solita had come to town looking for more than a new restaurant. She needed a new beginning. Her only son, a teenager named Buddy, had just died of cancer. The grief almost killed her, until she finally decided to fight. Her daughter and son-in-law owned a hotel in town. She thought opening a restaurant next to it would be a good business move, but more than that, it would keep her too busy to give in to her pain. It was no cure. Her misery still clung jealously to her insides, but she had learned to wear it like an invisible shroud as she pursued this new venture.

When I saw her that first time, she made the usual impression on me that new faces do. I was a pretty shy kid, but people have always been interesting to me. I wondered about them, and I wondered what they thought when they looked at me.

In the south, Segregation had made such a mess of things that something as simple as eye contact between people of different races was an awkward, sometimes humiliating, even occasionally dangerous undertaking. It would have been easier to size a person up from a list of stereotypes and go on about your business, than to make any attempt to connect. That was the choice a lot of people—black and white—opted for. It was not the one for me.

I wasn't blind to the racial tension in Eufaula and so many other cities. I believed in justice and understood that while I lived in "the land of the free," there were few truly free people in a segregated world. Fear and ignorance gripped some, anger and bitterness owned others.

I knew that in the course of a day's work, I was smiling at some people who assumed that all black people were stupid, evil, or lazy. I knew that some of them hated me because their fathers and mothers had taught them to hate me. However, I also knew that some of *them* were hated, and seen as evil, lazy, and stupid. I had friends whose parents were raising them to distrust all white people. I could see even at my age that the door of racism swung both ways.

I decided that I wanted people to see *me* when they looked at me, not a color or a stereotype. I wanted to be liked—or hated—for who I was, not for who I wasn't. It could have been my mother's influence, I'm sure that was at least part of it. Somewhere in my brief number of days on this earth, I learned that you needed to become the kind of person you wanted others to be to you.

I couldn't live in the segregated south, demand to be seen and appreciated for who I was, and then act like a different person altogether. I had a good life, a family who loved me, work that motivated me, and no real problems. I was happy and grateful. I had joy and dreams and others to care for. I was a good student in school. I was not hopeless or angry. It truly didn't occur to me that there were limits on me then, because I had always been able to do those things that really mattered to me. I decided that this was the boy people should see when they encountered me. What they thought or did after that would be up to them. If they were determined to hate me, I couldn't do anything about that...but I could give them a choice. That was the boy who smiled at Solita Horton from the kitchen of the Drive 'Round It.

Miss Solita would tell me many years later that when she saw me that first time, there was something in my smile that caused her grief over Buddy to just melt away. Like everybody who came into the restaurant, she saw *me*; happy to be doing what I was doing, certain that life meant me no harm. I was too young to know that you could suffer enough to lose all your joy. I had never seen the bottom of my supply of it, so I spent it prodigally, extravagantly and excessively, and most of it came out in my smile.

There were no walls between black boys and white women that day. We were, from that divinely instigated first encounter, mother finding son, sorrow clinging to joy, innocence meeting insight. We were The Prodigal and The Practical both with much to teach and to learn from one another. She adopted me that day into her heart. This tiny white woman, who needed to place a phone book on her chair to sit comfortably behind the cash register at the counter, became one of the giants in my life.

My own mother had taught me how to cook. Miss Solita introduced me to gourmet food. Ours was a wonderful pairing. She would take me to nice restaurants and then we would return to her restaurant, The Town House, and experiment on duplicating and improving on those dishes. She taught me how to dance and helped me buy my first suit for the prom. She's the reason I began to think about going to college.

I served her as best I could and I am convinced that we were necessary and precious gifts to each other. A quote from C.S. Lewis' "The Problem of Pain" reminds me of my time with this special woman.

"Love is something more stern and splendid than mere kindness."

My friendship with Miss Solita could have settled into the mere kind exchange of pity; me for her as a grieving mother, her for me as a poor colored boy living in Alabama. But there is something about sincerely giving yourself to another person over time that relegates pity to the stingiest of offerings. Over time, if there is real love between people, the spectacular dance of vulnerability and strength becomes the ministry connecting them to each other.

I think if I had not met this brilliant, generous woman; if we had not chosen to build trust through the sharing and bearing of one another's burdens, our lives would be very different. Mine surely would be the poorer without her.

Dr. Thomas Vivian McCoo—known to most as Dr. T.V. McCoo—practiced medicine in Eufaula for 50 years. He was a distinguished black man with kind quiet eyes and a pleasant manner. He was soft-spoken and very humble, yet he still managed to inspire trust and confidence in his patients and respect in and beyond our community.

Dr. McCoo began coming to The Town House shortly after I started working there. He and Miss Solita were friends. One day he saw me and asked me if I knew how to make oyster stew. It was simple enough, and I was a little surprised that this man who could eat anything wanted oyster stew, but I made it for him.

After that, more often than not, Dr. McCoo would stop by the restaurant and I would cook up a bowl of oyster stew for him. He seemed content to eat it in the kitchen with me, so I prepared a place for him. I would stack a couple of crates on top of each other, then put newspaper over them as a makeshift tablecloth, and set out napkins and a spoon. We talked while he ate while I cooked and cleaned up. He answered all my questions and engaged me with some questions of his own.

Dr. McCoo impressed me from the beginning. He was our family doctor and he took care of most of the families in our neighborhood. He worked at the colored hospital because black doctors weren't allowed to work at white hospitals unless someone needed care and no white doctors were available. Even then, some white patients still refused to be seen by black doctors. That didn't stop Dr. McCoo. He succeeded despite the obstacles and enjoyed a well-earned reputation as one of the best doctors—black or white—in Eufaula.

More than half a century later, I can still see Dr. T. V. McCoo's imprint on my life. I have a gift of encouragement that I would not know about if it weren't for him identifying it and teaching me about the value of it. I waited on his words. There is something that lives deep within the human soul which seeks for confirmation that we are on this earth for a reason; that we matter. Dr. McCoo recognized and called out that part of me until it began to declare itself on its own.

It was not unusual for him to interrupt one of our conversations and say something like, "Solomon, don't ever lose that smile. It's good for the soul," or "Never stop dreaming Solomon. You can do anything you set your mind to." Then he would elaborate on his particular exhortation and entertain any questions or comments from me.

Throughout his life and sometimes in the psalms he wrote King David found himself humbled at the attention God paid him. We find him asking God, "Who am I that You take notice of me, and not only notice me, but You concern Yourself with my wellbeing, receive from my hand, and visit me the way a friend visits another, with conversation and listening." (2 Sam. 7:18, 1 Chron. 17:16, 29:14, Ps. 8:4)

I have feelings similar to those when I think of Dr. McCoo. He didn't have to spend time with me. He had a son of his own who was more like him than I was. (He would eventually become a doctor like his father.) He had more than a few obligations and responsibilities. Who was I that he would let me entertain him with a bowl of stew and my adolescent conversation? I knew he was an important man in our community, and he treated me like I was an important person in his world. He talked, but more than that, he listened to me. He told me about his life, but he seemed to be more interested in helping me shape mine. Who was I? I believed then as I do now, that I was the most fortunate person I knew.

He was a great man. When he died, the editor of the local newspaper wrote, "Not only was Dr. McCoo a competent physician who rendered invaluable service to the suffering, but equally as important he was a dedicated civic and religious leader for many years…Eufaulians of both races have lost a friend."

∾ ∿

Wisdom is the willingness to make the choices that give you the freedom to be good and to do good for others. It's different from intelligence in that it doesn't allow us to become arrogant which is the probable outcome of the simple accumulation of knowledge. There is a Japanese proverb that declares, "Knowledge without wisdom is a load of books on the back of an ass." Moreover, real wisdom is always constructive. It always builds up, whereas knowledge, if it's paired with wrong motives, can be destructive.

Wisdom is distinguished from emotional maturity because feelings—even healthy ones—are not actions, and as I mentioned earlier, wisdom is nothing if it's not active.

Thirdly, and probably most important, wisdom is not merely willpower, because it's not generated from within us. We are born with a will, but not wisdom. If we had been born with wisdom—even a little bit—right living, obedience, kindness, forgiveness, maturity, and success would come to us naturally. There would be no greed, cruelty, pride, fear, envy, or insecurity in us, because we would know from birth what was good not only for us, but for others, and we would always make the choices to live that out. One look at the evening news proves we are not born wise.

As human beings, we all possess an intellect, emotions, and a will. Wisdom, though separate from each of those parts of us, calls each of them into its service daily, loudly and clearly, but patiently and without forcing the issue. There is a significant difference between finding wisdom and being wise.

Solomon began his life searching for wisdom. If you examine his life, you will see that while he continually discovered it, and wrote about it, he didn't always use it. Walking out our lives as wisdom directs us is not always the most comfortable undertaking. However, as he neared the end of his life, Solomon came to the conclusion that as in marriage (for better or worse, for richer or poorer, in sickness and in health, and let me add "in pain" and "in pleasure" to that), wisdom requires our commitment in order for us to realize the true beauty of it and joy in it.

I hope as we walk together that you will see what God showed Solomon, an image of wisdom anxious to be known and loved; cherished the way a woman longs to be cherished by her husband. He is the author of the eighth chapter of Proverbs in the Bible. Look at the following excerpt from The Message translation:

> *"I am Lady Wisdom, and I live next to Sanity;*
> *Knowledge and Discretion live just down the*
> *street…Good counsel and common sense are my*
> *characteristics; I am both Insight and the Virtue*
> *to live it out. With my help, leaders rule, and*

lawmakers legislate fairly. With my help, governors govern, along with all in legitimate authority.

"I love those who love me; those who look for me find me. Wealth and Glory accompany me—also substantial Honor and a Good Name. My benefits are worth more than a big salary, even a very big salary; the returns on me exceed any imaginable bonus.

"You can find me on Righteous Road—that's where I walk—at the intersection of Justice Avenue, handing out life to those who love me, filling their arms with life—armloads of life!

"GOD sovereignly made me—the first, the basic—before He did anything else. I was brought into being a long time ago...Before Mountains were sculpted and Hills took shape, I was already there, newborn; Long before GOD stretched out Earth's Horizons, and tended to the minute details of Soil and Weather, and set Sky firmly in place...I was right there with him, making sure everything fit. Day after day I was there, with my joyful applause, always enjoying His company...

"So, my dear friends, listen carefully...those who embrace these my ways are most blessed...don't squander your precious life. Blessed the man, blessed the woman, who listens to me, awake and ready for me each morning, alert and responsive as I start my day's work.

"When you find me, you find life, real life, to say nothing of GOD's good pleasure."

What an amazing invitation! I have spent the better part of my life taking this Lady up on her offer, and I have never been disappointed. She came after me, before I knew I needed her, through those who had already discovered her treasure. Through them I came to know her. Now, many years, and many home runs and hard knocks later, I have my own gray hair, a few wrinkles and lots of stories to tell about my time with her.

I have enjoyed most of the promises of Proverbs 8. There is nothing left for me to do but light the way for others to enjoy them too. I realize that somewhere on my journey, I became that spring that I sought in my youth, anxious to release to others what I have been given…a love for wisdom and a desire to draw others into the spectacular pursuit of her. I hope you will continue on with me.

You Are Here. Where Exactly is "Here"?

WISDOM is the willingness to make the choices which give you the freedom to be good and do good for others.

At Wisdom's feet is where we will begin our journey together. She lives wherever you make your home. Remember, she's pursuing you, even when you can't see her. She becomes visible the moment you desire to know her beyond a casual acquaintance. Now that you know where she is, and she knows where you are, the only question left to answer is: Do you know where you are?

If I were looking for you today, at this moment, where would I find you? Where are you on your emotional, spiritual, psychological, professional, relational, and familial maps? How content are you? How clear are you about what you want, what you believe, and why you care about what matters to you?

Look at the following table and complete the phrases by checking the box which best describes you. As you consider each one, scribble any thoughts or feelings in the margins of these pages if they occur to you. Spend as much time on each one as you need to. If you want to ask someone you trust for input, do it. You're fortunate that you have people to call on.

Above all, be honest. Even and especially if your eyes are

the only ones that will see what you write, it's important that you remain as truthful as you can throughout this process. If you try to read a map from a false starting point, your chances of getting where you want to go will be pretty slim.

	A	B	C
When I look at myself, I see...	☐ Ugly	☐ Flawed	☑ Beautiful
In my skills/ gifts, I am...	☑ Insecure	☐ Competent	☐ Confident
If others get what I wanted, I feel...	☐ Envious	☑ Nothing	☐ Happy
My childhood has left me...	☐ Damaged	☐ Hurting	☑ Prepared
When caught lying, I'm...	☐ Defensive	☐ Ashamed	☑ Responsible
When it's "just me," I am...	☐ Lonely	☐ Alone	☑ Content
When I want my way, I...	☐ Control	☐ Persuade	☑ Influence
On my job, I feel like a...	☐ Prisoner	☑ Student	☐ Leader
I would grade my life...	☐ Failing	☑ Passing	☐ Excellent

Column A: If you have answers in this column, you need a CHAMPION, that is, someone in your corner to tell you the truth about yourself. Discouragement, the scars of abuse or neglect, fear of rejection, a broken heart, shame, and powerlessness can put us in this place, and paint a false picture of who we are and what we're capable of.

Column B: If you have answers in this column, you're not in a bad place, but you do need a CHALLENGE to get/keep you moving in the right direction. In this place it's easy to become complacent, or become satisfied with feeding your ego instead of satisfying your soul. People in this place can feel restless or frustrated with their lives and not be able to put their finger on why. It's not your imagination. Something inside you needs stirring up to keep you from falling into Column A.

Column C: If you have answers in this column, you're doing well, but that doesn't mean your work is done. You need a CHARGE or a set of marching orders. There are people who need to learn what you have to teach, hear what you have to say. You have overcome some things, and now it's time for you to help some others come over too. They are around you, in your path, calling out to you. Your assignment is to pay attention and respond.

WHERE HAVE WE FOUND YOU AND WHAT DO YOU NEED?

Write down where you are in your life. What do you see today that you didn't see before? What is standing out to you right now? Do you need a champion, a challenge, or a charge? Perhaps you need more than one. Ask for it now. Write down everything that comes to your mind, generalities and specifics, emotions or random ideas. Don't edit yourself. Don't just think about it, write it down. That will cause you to focus in the moment, and later, when other things are crowding into your head, you can go back to these pages and remember.

When evaluating myself, I feel as though there are a few things that come to mind that I need help with. I really have never had a problem w/ being confident in the way God has made me. I know that I am beautiful & I know that I have been favored in the area of looks. However, sometimes, I fall into the Category of False Humility, because If someone comes up to me & say somethin like "you look good," I'll act shy about it. My Childhood didn't really damage me or hurt me, but I feel as if it didn't prepare me fully for life's challenges. I had to learn how not to be like my father, & how to show my family as well as my brothers & sisters that it is possible to live life & enjoy it. Everyday is a learning process for me, God has placed me around some men who truly love God, their wives, & their children, & I thank God for catching me up in that area. When it comes down to skills, I feel insecure a lot of times, because when I sit down & try to think of specific skills that I'm good at, it's very hard for me. Outside of sports, there is nothing that I Can remember ever being taught & developed in to become better at it. This frustrates me, because I know there has to be life for me outside of sports, I have a passion for business & Entrepreneurship, but I know that I need to be developed in those areas.

CHAPTER TWO

Winner By Design

*Esteem [Wisdom], and she will exalt you;
embrace her, and she will honor you.*
                    –SOLOMON (PROVERBS 4:8)

*Success is not to be pursued; it is to be
attracted by the person you become.*
                    –JIM ROHN

*Success is not hiding from any of us. It is
waiting for all of us, no matter who we are or
how we started out in life, as long as we are
willing to be shaped by our circumstances.*
                    –SOL HICKS

❧ ❦

I had one brother whose name was Moses. He was
tragically murdered in 1980 in Chicago. He was just 33
years old and he left a wife and two small children behind.
I still miss him when I think of him. He was one of those
guys who didn't know everybody, but everybody knew
him. Moses was funny and friendly, a smooth talker and a
sharp dresser. He was the first truly confident friend I had.

He wasn't your average clumsy teenage boy. He didn't have any trouble talking to girls or receiving their attention. When he entered a room, he expected the atmosphere to change; and it usually did.

I used to worry about him sometimes because he would talk about wanting to walk in the front door of one of the restaurants in town, seat himself at the counter and order some lunch. In those days, that could get a black man in Alabama arrested or worse. We both knew that, but Moses would go on about how he had just as much right to eat at that counter as anyone else. My brother was bold, but he was also a thinker. He was a little radical, but he had courage and he made a lot of sense.

Moses knew who he was and celebrated rather than apologized for it. He had a very powerful personality; he believed that he was worth knowing, and that his impression was worth leaving on the world. I admired that about him. As a boy, I used to want to be like him, but my personality seemed to resist all of my efforts to transform it.

I was sort of the "anti-Moses" growing up. I didn't have lots of friends my age to hang out with. I hung out at work. Besides Moses, my "posse" was my mom, my grandmother, Miss Solita, Dr. McCoo, and a few of the old people in our neighborhood. There was no one more naïve or more socially unskilled than I was. I could cook and clean, but I couldn't shoot a basketball or hit a baseball, barely dated, and forget about dancing. Even today, my up-tempo moves are at best an embarrassment and at worst a danger to anyone without a hardhat or steel-toed boots. My daughters have made it abundantly clear to me that I am "challenged" in that area.

I would have expected a book like this one to be written

by Moses, or at least someone very much like him.

Isn't that what many of us believe? Success happens for those who talk faster, look better, communicate with more confidence, know what they want, and have a plan to get it. Those are the men and women who write the books and give the talks on making the most of your life because they are the ones who appear to make the most of theirs. These are not your average walkers through this world. They are the ones who swagger, glide, fly, or push. They don't ask for permission, they give it. They are never told to "get out of the way." They *are* the way, and their way is studied, picked apart, and consumed by the fumbling, halting, and faltering of this world who'll settle for just of piece of that highway.

The anatomy of our thinking goes something like this: We're born at a point in history to a particular family with a specific set of circumstances. We're equipped with a measure of Pretty and/or Ugly, a personality, a set of coping skills, a mental capacity, and a certain amount of drive. All this, plus our experiences, determine how successful we can or can't become. Success, from this lens, is a profile we either fit or don't fit to varying degrees.

Let me meet you in that head. Think about where you are right now and answer this question: If success were a crime, would there be enough "evidence" of it in your life to convict you? Take a minute to think about that. Now go stand in front of a mirror or close your eyes and imagine you are in front of one. You see that guy? You see that woman? THAT'S ALL THE EVIDENCE YOU NEED.

Go back to the questions in our introduction:

- Are you living the life that daily answers the deepest desires of your heart? Do you know what those desires are?

- Is your life bigger than your own imagination and greater than people's expectations?

- Do you know what you were sent here to say to the world through your particular set of circumstances? Do you have the courage to devote your life to saying it, no matter what it costs you?

- Can you see the tools that God has placed at your feet to help you discover every promise He made to you before He breathed life into you?

- Are you ready to live exceeding abundantly beyond all that you could ask or even think?

By the time you finish reading this book, I want you to be able to answer all of those questions affirmatively. If that's going to happen, I need to plant something in you, if it isn't already there, before you go on.

Success is yours for the taking... if you want it.

There is nothing that can disqualify you from success. That's not just some positive declaration for you to meditate on, stick to your bathroom mirror or place on your desk at work. Part of living out our purpose on earth is discovering what we were put here to teach by learning and paying special attention to the lessons that repeat themselves in our lives. My life teaches what I have learned over and over again and what I hope to communicate within these pages—that success is not hiding from any of us. It is waiting for all of us, regardless of who we are or where we've been, as long as we are willing to be shaped by our circumstances.

I don't know whose eyes are falling upon these words.

I don't know if you're just passing time with me or if you're really looking for some answers. Maybe you've got a great life and you're just curious about what you have in common with somebody who thinks he's got a life that's great enough to write about. If that's your story, I'm happy to know you and thrilled that your life is working out well. I hope this read is a confirming and encouraging experience for you.

However, I also hope to say something to those of you who are struggling in your work, with your spouse, in ministry, or at school. I want a word with that man or woman who has fallen so many times that getting up one more time just doesn't seem worth the trouble. I want your attention if you're at the point where you'd just settle for making ends meet, getting a good night's sleep, or feeling competent at your job. If you are or have ever been discouraged, bitter, joyless, confused, angry, envious, miserable, or tired, don't stop reading. If you're going to bed and waking up afraid that this is all there is, don't worry. It isn't.

It's not too late for you. You *are* good enough. You do matter. There are people who need to learn what you have to teach. This space you're in isn't The Place, it's a place on the way to The Place.

Getting everything you want requires understanding that success is not something you ever have to chase; it's something you only need to learn to expect and accept. It's not the possible result of good behavior, but the inevitable fruit of wise living.

That is a simple yet very powerful statement, but if you can get it into your spirit—if you can set about weaving it into the very fabric of your soul—you will be free to live the life you've always desired.

I know you want success. We all do and there's nothing wrong with that. In fact, I think there's something wrong if we don't want to succeed at something. However, if you just want it and you're looking for a way to focus, or walk out a process to achieving it, I'm not the guy you want to hear from. I'm the guy who wants to get you to the place where you move beyond a simple desire for success to *knowing* it as a part of your very person and personality.

The reason I refer to success as fruit you're designed to bear, as opposed to a goal you have to get, is because goals, which are apart from you, are dependant on what you do to move toward them. Fruit is *inside* a tree or a vine from the day it takes its first breath. It is the "natural" result of normal growth.

Foundational to everything I believe is the assumption that it is not in God's nature or ability to fail. He doesn't plan for failure, make contingency for it, expect it, or even consider it, because it is the one thing that's impossible for Him. He didn't design anything to fail. Failure is something we chose in the Garden of Eden with that first act of disobedience, but it is not something we were designed for. "Successful" is how we were created and successful is how we could have continued if we had wanted God to have His way.

Look at everything God created without a free will. None of it is designed to fail either in its operation or in its relationship to all other things. When it does, 100% of the time, that failure is traceable back to man.

Intention always precedes creation. God had a plan when he designed us all as Humanity, and each as individual human beings. Each of us is designed to succeed at who we are, and every element of our experience and environment was designed to move us closer to success.

My brother Moses was designed for a different life than I was. I'm living the life that I was designed to live, the one that answers desires that were placed in my heart the moment God placed me in my mother's womb. Whatever challenges that come with being who I am, where I'm from, what I have or don't have, were designed to equip me for success, not bar me from it. Let me refer you to another Moses to make my point.

> *Moses was tending the flock of Jethro his father-in-law, the priest of Midian, and he led the flock to the far side of the desert and came to Horeb. There the angel of the LORD appeared to him in flames of fire from within a bush…God called to him from within the bush, "Moses! Moses!"… [He] said, "I am the God of your father, the God of Abraham, the God of Isaac and the God of Jacob…I have indeed seen the misery of my people in Egypt…So I have come down to rescue them from the hand of the Egyptians and to bring them up out of that land into a good and spacious land, a land flowing with milk and honey…So now, go. I am sending you to Pharaoh to bring my people the Israelites out of Egypt."*

God had a plan for Moses. If you look at his history, Moses was born at a time when all the newborn sons of Hebrew slaves were being killed because the Hebrews were beginning to outnumber the Egyptians. However, Moses lived. In fact, he grew up in Pharaoh's house, raised as the son of Pharaoh's daughter, who hired, of all people, his own biological mother to nurse and nurture him! When everyone in his same circumstance was dying, he was spared, because it was in line with God's plans, never mind anyone else's.

So let's understand this. God allows a man to be born while everyone around him who is like him is dying. He gives him safety and a secure upbringing in an Egyptian home, but develops in him a Hebrew heart. Do you think anyone but the household of Pharaoh could have broken Pharaoh's law and let that Hebrew baby live? Then many years later, do you think Moses would have gotten in to see Pharaoh and deliver God's message without being killed if he hadn't grown up as the man's "grandson"? It's doubtful.

The plan God has for our success is more than a promise down the road. It's our protection on the road (more about that in a later chapter). Winning is not just a part of His idea, it is the whole idea! Notice that God lays out what success looks like *before* He tells Moses that he's the guy who's being sent. That's because God doesn't wonder if He's going to win. He's certain of it, and if we're with Him, living out His objectives for us, we don't have to waste our time wondering either. It's that certainty that we stand on so we don't lose heart even when it seems like we're losing ground. Yes, I am saying what you think I'm saying. Winning is the foolproof plan of God for all of us.

The logical (and very human) question that follows is if that's true, why do so many of us fall short of it? Why isn't everyone having a great life? Why isn't winning the rule? Why is it the exception if it's not just for the exceptional? In short, WHY IS SUCCESS SO DARN HARD?

It's hard because the heart of true success—the indispensable, unchangeable and irrevocable part of it—requires us to commit ourselves to wisdom, and that requires us to submit ourselves to it. Wisdom is the revelation of the intentionality of God. It is His way of finding us, wherever we are, and showing us how to win in that place and from that place. Loving wisdom means progressively increasing in our ability to see the heart, head, and hand of God, then choosing, moment by moment, to align our own heart, head, and hands with His. Wisdom is the revealed path of Someone who knows, better than we do, what we should do, and where we should go; in other words, how we should live. When we have real success, the kind that comes through wise living, we don't just have the desires of our hearts. We have also learned along the way to have the right desires, the ones that lead to our *being good and doing good for others.*

The reason most of us don't realize that kind of success, the reason we settle for just enough to impress people, or we give up trying, is because most of us are expecting to be responsible for making it happen when we're really only responsible for letting it happen. What's the difference? Let's look at Moses again:

> *But Moses said to God, "Who am I, that I should go to Pharaoh and bring the Israelites out of Egypt?" And God said, "I will be with you. And this will be the sign to you that it is I who have sent you: When you have brought the people out of Egypt, you will worship God on this mountain." Moses said to God, "Suppose I go to the Israelites and say to them, 'The God of your fathers has sent me to you,' and they ask me, 'What is his name?' Then what shall I tell them?" God said to Moses, "I am who I am. This is what you are to say to the Israelites: 'I AM has sent me to you.' Go, assemble the elders of Israel and say to them... 'I have watched over you and have seen what has been done to you in Egypt. And I have promised to bring you up out of your misery in*

Egypt into...a land flowing with milk and honey.'
The elders of Israel will listen to you. Then you and
the elders are to go to the king of Egypt...But I know
that the king of Egypt will not let you go unless a
mighty hand compels him. So I will stretch out my
hand and strike the Egyptians with all the wonders
that I will perform among them. After that, he will
let you go. And I will make the Egyptians favorably
disposed toward this people, so that when you leave
you will not go empty-handed." (Exodus 3)

Are you looking at this argument? Moses says, "Don't you want somebody special for this?" God says, "You're somebody special to Me, and I'm special, and this is what it's going to look like when you and I win. Oh, and by the way, the Egyptians—the people in charge down there— they're going to fight us on this, but that won't change my plans any. They're going to lose, lose big, *and* they're going to like it!" You'd think that would be the end of the matter, Moses would say, "When do we leave?" and God would give him his itinerary. But no, the argument doesn't stop there. Moses has a few more things to say in Exodus 4, and God patiently repeats that success is Plan A and there is no Plan B. Then comes the big showdown.

But Moses said, "O Lord, please send someone else
to do it." Then the LORD's anger burned against
Moses...

Do you want to know why success is the exception and not the rule? Because the "unexceptional" don't want to play by the rules, that's why. When we're faced with the fact that real success is always bigger than we are; when we grasp that it's going to require commitment rather than control, most of us shrink away from it. Then we rationalize our decision (that is we tell *rational lies*). Most of us convince ourselves, like Moses did, that our own lack of ability, credibility, or believability is the problem, when in actuality, it is precisely our awareness of own our lack that sets us up to win. It's only when we are convinced of it that we are ready to make use of all the advice, instruction, and tools available to us. That's wise living, and it's only possible for those who understand that they need it.

You are that woman or that man handpicked to succeed. There is no Plan B. If Moses had decided not to obey God, there was no "Back-up Deliverer." Your life is yours to live or no one lives it. If you don't succeed, there is no one to succeed for you. You are the only one alive who can say what you have to say, do what you have to do, touch the lives you were made to touch. "Send somebody else"? There is nobody else!

I don't want to teach you how to live my life. You've got yours to live. I want you to know that it is worth living no matter what it looks like right now. I don't just believe that. I was designed to help you believe it not just for your sake but for the sake of everyone who will ever know you or know of you.

Author George MacDonald said, "Every one of us is something that the other is not and therefore knows something—it may be without knowing that he knows it—which no one else knows: and...it is everyone's business...to give his portion to the rest."

The plan for your life is never about what can happen to you, but what can happen *through* you. Think about that image of fruit again. Humanity was designed to "be fruitful and multiply." In the story of The Creation, fruit appears on the third day, before we do, to give us a picture of what successful humanity should look like. We were made to reproduce the way fruit trees or vines do.

Have you ever seen a tree picking its own oranges, or a vine plucking its own grapes? Have you ever seen the plants of an orchard watering or pruning themselves? Do they cause the winter or spring to come? Can they keep the parasites off of their own leaves? Can they ever decide how much fruit will appear or direct their branches to hold onto it if the wind blows or a hungry stranger passes by?

Fruit is the natural and inevitable product of healthy, living plants. When we are fruitful, we confirm our value to the world, and by feeding others, add value to their lives. Because we were not designed to fail, we can decide to thrive wherever we're planted. We can decide to allow every event or involvement to water and nourish us, bask in the joy of summer, or find rest in the sorrow of our winters, and we can learn to enrich others with the gift of ourselves. Then, success becomes our inheritance and the legacy we leave. In other words, wherever you are—up, down, sitting pretty, falling behind, or giving up—your next step and every one after it will reveal, for as long as you opt to see it, an occasion to be good or to do good. Choose wisely. After all, what good is a tree that won't bear its own fruit?

What did God intend when He made you? If you don't know, it's time you found out. If you do know, let every selection you make from here on out give greater light your path and light the way for others as you live into your unique harvest.

Inner Space

I have been handpicked to succeed. My life is mine to live or no one lives it. No one can succeed for me. I am Plan A and there is no Plan B. Only I can say what I have to say, do what I have to do, touch the lives I was made to touch.

Read this paragraph a few times. What thoughts and feelings come up as you reflect on those words?

Think and write about 1 habit you wish you didn't have, 2 strengths people don't realize you have, and 3 lessons you can teach.

I know that there is something so dynamic that God wants to do through me that will impact the World. I have no doubt that it will happen, because God has already spoken it over my life. I feel very blessed God would choose me to fulfill a part of this plan. I thank God for all He's done for me + all that He is going to do through me. One habit I wish I didn't have is not being able to effectively manage + maximize my time everyday. Two strengths people don't realize I have is my ability to motivate people & inspire them to dream again. Secondly, I believe I have a keen ability to point people in the direction that they should be going. I can easily locate what a person's passion is & how they should be doing something just by having a conversation with them. Three lessons I can teach would be ① The Importance of having the right people surrounding you. ② The power of speaking the word of God over your life. ③ Your past does not have to dictate your future. (How you grew up, where you came from, etc.)

CHAPTER THREE

At First Sight

Above all else, guard your heart, for it is the wellspring of life.

—SOLOMON (PROVERBS 4:23)

The question is not what you look at, but what you see.

— HENRY DAVID THOREAU

Seeing is what happens when you know the truth about what you're looking at, even if it's invisible.

—SOL HICKS

❧ ❦

I have been married to my wife Carol for 43 years at this writing. I'm still deliriously in love with my exquisite bride, and she still flirts with me and thinks I'm wonderful (at least that's what she tells me).

I asked Carol to marry me the day I met her.

I'm certainly not the first guy to do that. History tells the story of World War I British Navy Commander Edward Ratcliffe Evans, nicknamed "Evans of the Broke," who, on a visit to Oslo, was seated next to a blonde woman at a dinner party. Before they had finished the first course, he turned to her and said, "Do you like soup?" Receiving her answer, he replied, "Nether do I—let's get married." She accepted and their marriage was said to have been a happy one. That's impressive, but I wonder how the commander would have responded if his Nordic crush had turned him down.

Carol turned me down that first day...and for 85 days after that.

I was an agent with Prudential Insurance for 35 years. During that time, I won more trophies, awards, and honors than I can count. I'm retired now, but I continue to spend a fair amount of time consulting; advising the agents that I mentor, meeting and corresponding with others, and speaking at agencies all over the world. I like to tell stories about my work. That's not hard for me. Anytime you spend three and a half decades in a profession as peopled as selling life insurance, stories are never in short supply. That said, however, when I'm asked, as I often am, to tell the story of my first successful sale, I usually reach back to before my time at Prudential, and I talk about proposing to Carol.

I was 20 years old and I had just left Kansas City where I had been living with my father and his wife. The relationship with my stepmother was strained. She wanted and didn't have children. Maybe I was salt in that wound. Maybe I was a reminder that my father had loved before. I wasn't sure, and it didn't matter. I decided the best thing for me to do was leave. I chose to go into the armed services. I tried all of them—army, navy, air force—and was turned down by all of them because I have flat feet. Disappointed, I went to visit my grandmother in Chicago. Once there, I was informed by my stepmother back in Kansas City that

I was no longer welcome in her home. She didn't give a reason, and I didn't require one. Sometimes we have to figure out where to go next, and sometimes the next place finds us first.

I secured a job working at a Bank to support myself. I didn't know anyone other than my grandmother in Chicago, so I decided to look up the sister of a guy I had gone to school with back home. Her name was Mary, and she was gracious enough to receive me into her social circle, which made the transition to my new life a little easier.

One day Mary invited me to a party at her place. There I learned how to play a card game called Hearts. It was great fun, but Mary and her friends played the game with a twist. If you won a hand, you had to drink a quart of water. Fortunately—and unfortunately—I am very competitive. The joy of winning was short-lived when I realized that the bathroom was a little further down the hall than I would have liked. I moved toward it with great purpose, nothing distracting me. Luckily I made it without incident.

As I was making my way back to the front of the apartment, I began to pay attention to those things that were a blur just moments earlier. I passed by a room that I vaguely remembered and saw that the door was slightly ajar. The legs of a person sitting in a rocking chair were all that was visible. I quietly pushed the door open to see more.

When I saw Carol, I was motionless for one of those eternal minutes that just hangs there, suspended, staring at you for as long as it takes you to realize that something life changing is going on.

It wasn't what she looked like, though I thought then—and still think—that she was one of the most beautiful women I had ever seen. She was rocking someone's sleeping baby. (I found out later that her sister was at the party and had asked Carol to come along and baby-sit while the party was going on.)

If her attractiveness had been all that had my attention, I would have quickly rejoined the people in the living room. I was painfully shy around pretty girls. I was almost afraid of them. At 20 years old, the one girl I could dubiously classify as a girlfriend was more than a little frustrated with me because I had managed to avoid kissing her despite numerous blatant overtures. She had no idea that I was so clueless, I actually believed that kissing would get her pregnant.

"Hello, my name is Solomon Hicks."

"Hello."

"You're gonna be my wife."

She didn't even waste a reaction on me before she went back to rocking that baby in her arms. Okay, my line wasn't as smooth as the British commander's "Do you like soup?" but I really wasn't trying to impress her so much as inform her of the one thought that had begun to pulse in my otherwise petrified mind. I was as shocked as she was unimpressed, so I just stood there for a few seconds before I determined that I should go back to the party. I needed more information about my future wife than she was willing to give me, her name for instance.

My inquiries got me a name, Carol Collins, and an introduction to her sister Geneva. I told her that I had met Carol and that she didn't like me. Geneva didn't seem surprised or bothered by that news. I was saying anything that came into my mouth to buy time while I came up with a strategy. Finally I asked, "Do you like to cook?" Maybe she thought I was trying to get myself invited over or something, I don't know. She told me she didn't like to cook. "Well, do you like to eat?" I asked.

The next night I showed up at the Collins sisters' door with groceries. I cooked, and the three of us ate. Carol said nothing during the meal. Then Geneva left the table for something and I saw my chance.

"How's the food taste?"

"Fine."

"Marry me and this could be yours for a lifetime."

"No."

I didn't argue, beg, or try to cajole her. I just showed up the next night, cooked, proposed, got turned down again, and came back the next night. This went on for about three or four weeks before Geneva told me that I really didn't have a shot with Carol because she had a boyfriend. His name was Ben and he had followed her to Chicago from Mississippi. They had been dating for awhile and were practically engaged according to Geneva. "Invite him to dinner," I said mentally calculating groceries for four instead of three.

Ben was a nice guy. I liked him. I think he liked me too, but when Ben decided to make himself a regular at our evening meals, we both knew what was going on. I was trying to read him, looking for any edge that would gain me some ground, and he was trying to make it clear, as courteously as possible, that the prize I sought had already been claimed. We would eat and then have polite conversation to cover for the fact that we were each trying to be the last to go home. One night Carol got tired of entertaining our genteel tug-o-war, so she left the two of us sitting in her living room and went to bed.

Still I managed, with every visit, to sneak a proposal into her ear when nobody was around or listening. As soon as I saw the smallest opening, I went for it. She never flirted with me or showed me any affection. She would refuse me every time, but she wasn't telling me to stay away, even with Ben in the picture. It was a good sign.

The tide began to turn in my favor one day when Carol admitted to me that she was beginning to like me. (*Hallelujah!*) She told me she felt conflicted because Ben had followed her there all the way from Mississippi and she did still care about him too. I understood and suggested that at dinner that evening, she listen to both of our plans for a future with her.

I borrowed a suit from my brother Moses. His clothes were much hipper than mine were. I cooked a fancy meal designed to show off a little and tried to be funnier, smarter, and more charming than Carol had ever seen me. After dinner I presented her with my plans for our future together. I brought my bank book so she could see that I had been saving my money. I had written down a few projections and even showed her how long it would take for us to buy our first home.

I could see that Geneva was very impressed and that I had Carol's undivided attention. When I finished talking, I fixed Ben with my best serious look and said, "So Ben, what are your plans for Carol?" He wasn't angry or even perturbed. I think he actually appreciated me. "I don't have a plan like that," was all he said.

I proposed to Carol for 86 straight days. On the 87th day she said yes. The very next day, I took a bus down to Mississippi to ask her parents for her hand. On the way back I got the required permission from my own father in Kansas City (because I was under 21), and married Carol Collins before a Chicago judge after knowing her just 90 days.

Having Carol has made me grateful every day, but

pursuing her taught me something that I never forgot. Those 86 no's showed me one of the great differences between wisdom and knowledge. Knowledge will help you understand what you can and can't navigate, but wisdom will help you navigate what you can and can't understand. I learned that knowledge looks, but wisdom sees. Seeing is what happens when you know the truth about what you're looking at, even if it's invisible.

I knew Carol Collins would be my wife on the basis of nothing observable or reasonable. I didn't *feel* in love that first night, and it was obvious that she didn't. I had no evidence or information that suggested she would change her less-than-enthusiastic original opinion of me. She had a boyfriend, and she kept turning me down, not once, not five times, but *86 times*!

Normally, I have no trouble pointing to something and saying, "I don't get this. Would you explain it to me?" Carol was an altogether different thing. Instead of not seeing something that was there, I was seeing something that was not "there." I knew how to deal with someone who knew something I didn't, but this was a situation where I knew something that was hidden from everyone else.

Through that experience I learned to trust my discernment and looking back at my years with aged eyes, I realize that I've had it for most of my life. Some call it their "inner voice." For others, it's "a gut." For me it's a little more substantial than a voice in my head and more reliable than a feeling, but whatever you call it, it's a necessary tool for making wise decisions.

When Carol agreed to marry me, I was elated…but not surprised. I couldn't articulate it then, but I was certain that she and everyone else would eventually catch up to what I already knew was going to happen. It was like being shown the end of a book and then going back and reading each chapter with the rest of the class to see how the elements of the story get you all to that end.

People who are discerning are not special in the sense that they have something that only a few have access to. The opposite is true. The beauty of discernment is that it is inclusive and not exclusive in the way it operates. The Apostle Paul's words to the Corinthian church resonate for me:

> *Brothers, think of what you were when you were called. Not many of you were wise by human standards; not many were influential; not many were of noble birth. But God chose the foolish things of the world to shame the wise; God chose the weak things of the world to shame the strong. He chose the lowly things of this world and the despised things— and the things that are not—to nullify the things that are, so that no one may boast before him.*

I'm not the smartest guy in the room, far from it. I'm not a psychic, clairvoyant, mental marvel, prodigy, or a deep philosophical thinker. I'm discerning, and discernment is none of those things. I am confident when I move in a given direction, but my confidence comes from knowing I didn't conceive or construct the path. I just follow it. The root of the word success means "to go up," or "to follow after," meaning that a successful man or woman is one who moves toward something higher and better than what he or she has today. If wisdom is the path we follow to success, then discernment is having the eyes to see it especially when conventional understanding shows us a different way.

Discernment is like a muscle. We all have it, but if we don't use it, we lose the ability to use it. It works in conjunction with wisdom the way muscles work in a body. Your muscles don't atrophy from lack of use on their own. They are not capable of choosing inactivity any more than they can resist becoming fit if you choose a regular workout regimen. You exercise your discernment every time you see a wise choice and make it, and each wise choice improves your ability to discern others. Simply put, discernment is the ability to recognize what wisdom is trying to show you, but without decision it's weak. That's not deep, but if you embrace it, it is very, very powerful.

You don't need discernment to reach obvious conclusions. Work, shower before a first date, feed your pets, don't steal, call your mother, save some money, and don't leave your 4-year-old to baby-sit the 2-year-old are all wise choices, but people who have no discernment probably think that too. The value of a discerning heart is seen best when the obvious becomes invisible or the visible rejects the truth. When you have to find a way and there is no way lit, and what's at stake requires your urgent and immediate attention, discernment is vital. However if the discipline of it isn't already in place, you won't be able to make the most of it when you need it.

That's significant because everything you do is informed by what you believe you see, so if your discernment is darkened or damaged, it affects you and anyone attached to you. It influences your decisions, and how you handle every situation.

The greatest threat to your discernment is an unguarded heart. In other words, when you allow anything destructive to enter your belief system you are tampering with your ability to see the truth and act on it. Knowing this it's not hard to see why internet pornography eats away at some marriages, or why abusive parents raise kids who become abused and abusers.

If you're going to become all that you were put here to become, you must begin to take deliberate steps to guard your heart. You were not designed to fail. Remember that? Begin there and then look at everything in your life that contradicts that understanding. Start learning the truth and begin to look for opportunities to put that truth into action. As you become stronger, you can be more adept at communicating who you are to others, and forgive their offenses without accepting them. Guarding your heart means protecting it from anything that isn't contributing to you being good or doing good for others. It means turning off some television shows, putting down some magazines. It could mean not indulging some conversations or relationships.

Guarding your heart means keeping some things out, but it also means allowing beneficial things into it. How good are you at receiving the gift of friendship, encouragement, help, or constructive correction? Are there some wise men or women that you can observe and even ask for advice? When your heart is guarded, it's not withheld from loving others. It actually becomes more capable of loving, because good discernment sees more clearly how to care, but a blind heart can cost you and those around you dearly.

As I said, I was a pretty sheltered teenager. I didn't go out much. Most of my time was spent working for Miss Solita. At the end of each workday, I would walk the waitresses home while she closed up, and then she would drive me home. I usually had some time to kill so I walked over to the local theatre to see what movie was playing. I didn't go in, because it was a Whites Only establishment, but they had publicity photos from the films out front. I would look at those and try to imagine what the story inside was. I would create entire movies in my head. Years later when I saw the movies, they were never as exciting as I had envisioned them.

One evening, after seeing the ladies home, I took my usual walk over to the theatre. I was busy making movies in my head when a police car pulled up, shining its high beam lights directly on me. It took a second for my eyes to adjust enough to see the two white officers inside. By the time I did, they were out of the car.

Their business was obviously with me, but I had no idea what it was. I would have asked, but it wasn't necessary. One of them put his hand on his gun and said, "Run." Any thinking black boy in Alabama would be quick to put as much distance as possible between him and two armed white police officers. I'm no exception. I was terrified. Yet, something very still responded. "I won't run," I said quietly. "I didn't do anything." I was certain that if I ran, they were going to kill me. I thought if I was going to die, there would be no confusion about how it happened. I just stood there, close to tears, and they arrested me and took me to jail. I was booked on suspicion of robbery.

For the next few hours, I was locked up. They taunted me and called me things I will not put on this page. I was sure it was my last night on earth. I don't know if you've ever been resigned to dying. I imagine it must be the feeling a prisoner gets right before he's executed. This really is my last day, and these are my last breaths. After this there is nothing. I think it's the only time in my life I've ever *felt* dead. Then the miraculous happened.

They let me go. I don't know why. To be honest, I didn't care why. I didn't care about anything. I walked into the night air, and it didn't feel any fresher. I wasn't happy or relieved.

I wasn't free. I was out of jail, but something back at that awful place was still holding onto me. Everything looked right. I was walking on a dirt road, the way I did every night, but this had stopped being every other night four hours ago. I thought it would never be like any of those nights again. Something dark began to close down on my heart and I welcomed it.

When I didn't come back to the restaurant, Miss Solita started to worry. She came looking for me. I had decided to walk home. She pulled up alongside me and when I didn't stop walking, she called out to me, but I wouldn't turn around. I was too ashamed. "Solomon Hicks, get in this car!" The anger that had sustained me on the walk melted in the face of her concern. I got in. She didn't have to ask me what was wrong because we both knew I wasn't getting out until I told her. I had been demoralized and shamed and that's all I had to tell my story. It was enough.

Miss Solita spent the time it took to comfort and encourage me. She didn't take me home right away. Instead, she called her son-in-law and he went with us to the home of a judge in town. I couldn't believe what I was seeing. That tiny, woman banged on that man's door—at 3 a.m.—until he woke up and answered it. She told him what happened to me, told him who I was, and more importantly, told him who I was to her. The next day, those two officers were fired. What was most amazing though is what happened at the restaurant.

Miss Solita was well-known in Eufaula and The Town House was pretty popular. She introduced me to her friends when they came into the restaurant, and most of them knew her regard for me. It didn't take long for them to find out what happened, and many of them came into the restaurant to apologize. I was shocked when people I had only greeted and served up to that point, came into the restaurant and spoke directly to me, hoping I would not judge them or Eufaula by that horrible experience.

Discernment stopped me from running when reason told me that I was young, black, southern, and on the business end of a white policeman's loaded gun. Discernment caused Miss Solita to worry, and wait for me, then take action rather than let me sleep on my anger. I can't say if it was discernment or the fiery temper of his petite friend that made the judge act, but I'm grateful to him too.

The last and probably most significant thing to consider is this: The darkness that had threatened to envelope my heart that night was racism and bitterness. I knew I wasn't the first black boy, or man, or woman to be killed for sport by whites and I wouldn't be the last. Sure, I had been released, but I was hurt and I felt powerless. I couldn't do anything to those men, and I felt entitled to my rage, but when I saw how Miss Solita loved me—when my discernment showed me that all whites weren't automatically bad, just as I knew that all blacks weren't automatically good—the darkness was not welcome anymore.

My life has taken me all over the world, and I have met so many people. All of them are very different from me and each other. Getting to know them gives me pleasure I could never have imagined. If I had allowed myself to be robbed of that at 16, my life might be very different.

I wonder…

What things would I not have done because I couldn't see my way to them? Which parts of my story would be untellable?

Could a sullen, angry, racist boy continue to work for Miss Solita? Would a surly, enraged, bitter man have shown up at a card party, or noticed Carol Collins? And if he had, would he have asked 86 times for her hand? Would she ever have said yes?

I'm glad I don't have to wonder.

Take that, Evans of the Broke.

Inner Space

I am designed to succeed. I want to see opportunities to put that truth into action, and communicate it to others. I also want to be able to see everything and everyone that contradicts it and guard my heart.

Read this paragraph a few times. What thoughts, people, or feelings come up as you reflect on those words?

Think and write about **1** negative thought you want to stop replaying, **2** books you'd love to author, and **3** good qualities you always notice in others.

I know that God has made me & formed me to be a vital part in helping people's lives manifest what He has spoken over them. A lot of what God gives me is not for me, but for others to use so that they can get to where God needs for them to get. I take after my Spiritual father, Bishop L. Spenser Smith, in the sense that I am a destiny releaser. People need me to be who God has called me to be, so that I can be used to release them into who they need to be. One thought that I want to stop replaying is seeing myself as a normal person. I know that I am a Great person + God has greatness all over me. Three Good qualities that I notice in others is that ① Being well spoken + a great public speaker ② Confidence that challenges everyone + everything around to become who they need to become. ③ Being approachable is the third quality, because you may have all the wisdom of the ages, but people have to want to come up to you to recieve. Two books I'd like to author is tough, I'll have to get back to you on that one.

CHAPTER FOUR

Labor Pains

There is a time for everything...a time to be born and a time to die, a time to plant and a time to uproot, a time to kill and a time to heal...

—SOLOMON (ECCLESIASTES 3:1-3)

Birth is the sudden opening of a window, through which you look out upon a stupendous prospect. For what has happened? A miracle. You have exchanged nothing for the possibility of everything.

— WILLIAM MACNEILE DIXON

I wanted him to hurt since I was hurting... A steak knife was all I could find. It would have to do I thought. Then I realized that Carol was standing between me and the front door...She was demanding that I let go of the old man I was so desperate to protect and embrace the new one.

—SOL HICKS

Crimes of passion are never expressions of love, but of desperation. They erupt from the sudden and excruciating sense of vulnerability following a deep betrayal, when fear—like a fire set in the basement of the human heart— blinds us to everything but the reckless belief that we, and all we treasure, are threatened unless we take immediate and drastic action.

I have been truly desperate just once in my life. It was enough to convince me of two things. First, all thoughts— even dangerous ones—can seem reasonable in a panic. Second, if we're fortunate, someone will meet us in the midst of our frantic running about, and teach us the one lesson we must learn to keep from losing everything: We were never supposed to be our own heroes. When we are, we can never be more than the promises we keep...or don't keep.

"I'll buy your daughter a house within six months." That was the promise I made to Carol's mother when I asked for her hand; one I made good in just three months time working two jobs.

Monday through Friday, I was a bank teller during the day and at night I worked a graveyard shift at Johnson & Johnson, breaking up rosin with a sledgehammer, grinding it down, and then mixing it with starch, lanolin, and other materials necessary to make every kind of bandage. It was hard, physical labor, and my body was always tired, but I wouldn't take so much as a cat nap on my breaks for fear that the dust and chemicals which stuck to my clothes, skin, and hair would fuse my eyes shut.

I stopped by MacDonald's every morning after my shift at the factory to get a burger and a large soda, the latter because I needed the caffeine for my long drive. At home I would shower, exchange my dusty, sticky coveralls for a suit and tie and begin the second part of my usually 16-hour workday.

I had no real complaints. The routine was certainly taxing, but any discomfort was well eclipsed by the joy of being able to provide sufficiently for Carol and our daughter Cynthia. In fact I gratefully received as much overtime as J&J was willing to give me, and I would have continued that way, but a different path was imposed upon me.

One morning on the drive home, I fell asleep. I don't know when I closed my eyes or how far the car had driven without my attention or intention. I only know that I was snatched violently from that sweet slumber just one moment before it would have become permanent; a moment before my wife would be a widow and my child would be fatherless. A moment before everything that I cared about wouldn't be mine to care for anymore.

In what seemed like one ferocious movement, I smashed the brake with my foot, yanked the steering wheel in the opposite direction, and devoured the immediate landscape for approaching hazards as the car skidded to a stop.

Eventually, in the silence that now cocooned me, terror had given way to reasoning. This wasn't the first time I had fallen asleep at the wheel, just the first time it had almost killed me. I wasn't any more depleted than usual when I left work that morning. Then reasoning surrendered to understanding. How did I think I could push myself the way I was without consequences? Would I really kill myself just to prove I was a worthy husband and father. Was I actually willing to have Carol and Cynthia know me only as a eulogy?

Soberly I made my way home and told my wife what happened. We decided that one of the jobs would have to go. I spoke to my manager at the bank and explained my situation to him. He said if I went back to school and got a degree, he would promote me and give me a raise. On that promise, I enrolled at DePaul University. I knew things would be tight for a time, but the reward would be well worth the effort.

That first semester was hard. Studying, working fulltime, marriage, and fatherhood is a brutal juggling act. I anticipated fatigue, but the real challenge was seeing my family in that season of belt tightening, and resisting the urge to quit and take on another job just to relieve their discomfort.

Let me say here, that I don't know what marriage is like for the average person, but every time I think back on those days with Carol, I am almost always overwhelmed with gratitude. A lot is said about finding someone who can love you without conditions. But there is something incredible about a spouse who can love you *with expectation*, who's willing to water you well and often even before anything is showing above the ground.

I was helped so much at that time by Carol's certainty about who I was, and I could count on her, because I am blessed with one of those wives who doesn't see the value in lying to me just to flatter my ego. If she had thought I was a factory man, she would have gently told me not to bother with the bank. Instead, she simply expected me to work, study, husband, and parent when I often only suspected it was possible to do it all.

There was a deliberate effort being made to attract African American customers, and as the only person of color employed there with a "visible" position, I knew I was being groomed for more responsibility. The more I thought about my future, the more I enjoyed working at the bank. I could see my value. I would go in each day and imagine myself with that promotion. It made my heart light, and my smile bigger.

I was stunned the day my manager introduced me to the bank's newest hire. He was an ex-professional football player, moderately known around Chicago. Most of us recognized him and knew something about his career in the NFL. However, more significant to me than his past was his future. He had been hired to fill the position that had already been promised to me.

He was definitely more recognizable than I was, and would most certainly attract people to the bank. It was a good business decision even if it wasn't a moral one, but I couldn't see it as anything other than a vicious slap in the face. The frustration of all those nights wasted in class, studying until I couldn't see straight, regret over the time I *hadn't* spent with my wife and my child, and the shock as I witnessed the hope of making a better life for us suddenly dissolve, exploded inside me…and I quit.

The anger and the words were outside of me before I knew it, and I couldn't get them back. It was like that morning I fell asleep in the car, only this time I didn't wake up fast enough to keep from wrecking. I was sure they were wrong, but I remembered too late that being right doesn't pay a mortgage or buy milk, and my indignation soothed me only as long as it took to walk to the diner across the street.

What had I just done? How would I tell my wife that I had made a careless, selfish decision to put our family's wellbeing in jeopardy and there was nothing she could do about it? I had gone from having two jobs a few weeks ago to having no job. It didn't take long for discouragement to set up residence in me. I nursed a cup of coffee as misery eroded my confidence and drained me of any desire to see past my failure.

"Where's that smile I'm so used to seeing?"

I looked up and into the grinning face of Dan, an attorney whose account I managed at the bank. Dan and I spoke regularly. We chatted when he came in to do business and he commented often on how good I seemed to be at my job. Occasionally, I would call him if his balance couldn't cover a check that presented at the bank, and I'd let him know that he needed to make a deposit by the end of the day to keep it from being returned.

Today the tables were turned and Dan was asking how he could help me. I told him I had quit my job. I was looking for his grin to disappear and replace itself with a sympathetic expression or at least a frown of anger on my behalf. It didn't immediately change…and then it got wider.

"I think that's great," he said after a moment. When I asked him why, he didn't hesitate. "Come and work for me, Sol."

Dan explained to me that he made his money selling real estate and insurance, both home and life policies. He said he could really use someone like me and saw what happened to me as an opportunity for both of us. He had more leads than he could handle, so he would give me half of them, and we'd split whatever we made down the middle. I liked the idea that my income would be determined by how hard I worked as opposed to it being fixed no matter how hard I worked. We agreed to go into business together and I was excited.

I didn't know at the time that I needed a license to do

what I was doing. I didn't think about anything except how much I liked what I was doing. Dan was more a mentor than a business partner. He taught me everything he knew, congratulated me when I was successful, and encouraged me when I wasn't. He made sure I had all the materials I needed and showed me how to use them most effectively.

I saw myself changing. For the first time since I had moved to Chicago, it felt like I had a career and not just a job. I worked seven days some weeks because I enjoyed it and my level of confidence was so high even Dan couldn't believe the volume of business we were doing. He would say how much he was looking forward to getting paid for it. I agreed since I had all but depleted our savings waiting on those commissions.

Weeks became months and I was beginning to see why more people didn't work for themselves. Sure you didn't have the limits of salary, but entrepreneurship meant there was no regular paycheck in your inbox every two weeks. You were responsible for making the inbox and seeing that it got filled.

Saturday was one of those days I didn't have to go into the office, but usually did since so many of the people I worked with couldn't meet during the week because of their jobs. There was one particular Saturday that I didn't have anyone to meet, but I went in anyway. I decided to go through our invoices to see if I could bring closure to some of our outstanding accounts.

I started pulling out files. At first I wasn't sure that I was really seeing what appeared to be there. So I looked through more folders, and soon I began to feel sick to my stomach. One after another, the statements swam before my eyes. PAID...PAID... PAID...some with check numbers, others with copies of checks attached, but all of them had been paid, and all of the payments had been received by Dan…my partner, my mentor. My *friend* Dan had stolen—I added it up—$18,000.00 from me!

I called him at home. He was there and I told him what I had found. It didn't take him long to get to me. He hesitated for just a moment, and then he began to talk. I listened while he told me about his desperate financial situation. I listened to him apologize for lying to me and stealing from me. I listened to him beg for my patience and promise to pay me back. I listened, but I didn't hear what I wanted to hear. I didn't hear what my family was supposed to live on. I didn't hear why he thought it was all right to trample on my trust and my friendship. I didn't hear that he cared that I was devastated. I didn't hear how I was supposed to handle being a failure and a fool.

The basement of the human heart is where we keep all our personal "junk," the stuff we can't get rid of, but we're afraid to let other people see especially if it contradicts what we've invited them to look at. This is where we keep our mess-ups, our shame, cruelty, hopelessness, jealousy, bitterness, our fantasies of revenge, self-righteousness, and pain that won't go away.

This place is not, we believe, for public viewing. We're ashamed of it and what we think it says—or doesn't say—about us. I will welcome you to see that I'm a good person, successful, helpful, talented, and worthy of imitation. However, the door to my lower, "baser" self is locked and off limits to most.

Think about it. No one asks you over for dinner and says, "Follow me. We'll be dining underground tonight, on those smelly suitcases there. Let me put this mildewed blanket over them. We can use the stacks of yellowed newspapers for chairs, I'll serve your meal on that rusty paint can top, and we can sip wine from that old boot over in the corner. Oh yes, and the squealing of the rats that hide in the walls will be our entertainment." No, we eat where it is proper to eat, where things are at least tidy…and we hide the mess.

We're convinced that no one will react well to seeing our basement. The people who hate us will ridicule us, or gossip about us to the neighbors ("She's not as grand as she puts on, you know…"). The people who love us will feel sorry for us. ("I can't lean on him. He doesn't have it all together…"). We'll see that we are pitiful on their faces and in their actions.

Mind you, what they suspect is true. We are weak, and we should be pitied. The dirt, the mildew, the rusty paint cans, yellow newspapers, and old clothes are not figments of our imagination. The basement is real. It humiliates us and exposes our confidence as a façade. So we hide it because we are afraid that the one who hates us will exploit our weakness and hurt us. And we're equally afraid that the one we love will be afraid to trust us, and their trust is proof of our worth, the way company is proof that we have friends.

Dan had betrayed everything I believed about him. He had sharpened me and I had become more confident working with him. But he had used me, and was throwing me away. Everything he had taught me, said to me, encouraged or corrected me with was now questionable. I couldn't stand on it, much less walk in it. That job had consumed me and it had come to nothing…worse than that, I felt I had come to nothing.

I don't know how I made it to my car. Have you ever been so destroyed that you would have welcomed tears or pain or anything that would remind you that you weren't about to die? Everything that mattered to me was gone or crumbling to the ground. The vows I made to keep and care for my wife, and the promises I had made to her mother were about to shatter into a million unrecognizable pieces. I wasn't really afraid she would leave me, but the thought that she would not be able to trust me or be proud of me was crushing me.

My house was leveled, and the basement was all I had left. I would be weak to the man who betrayed me and pitiful to the woman who loved me…unless I did something about it. My plan wasn't reasonable. Desperate plans never are. I wanted him to hurt since I was hurting, and more than that, I wanted him to be weak while I was strong. I needed him to be afraid of me so that I would stop feeling so vulnerable.

I walked through the front door and covered the space to the kitchen with a couple of long strides. I rummaged quickly through drawers and cabinets. A steak knife was all I could find. It would have to do I thought. Weapon in hand, I turned to go the way I had come. Then I realized that Carol was standing between me and my exit.

I wasn't ready to talk to her, but she was clearly ready to talk to me. I tried to give her a look that said, "Don't ask me any questions. Just move out of the way and let me go." It wasn't fully formed on my face before she asked, "Honey, what happened?" She looked me in the eyes and calmly waited for my answer. I swear, if there had been no door or walls to keep me from the outside I still wouldn't have moved past her.

Something in her was calling out to something deep inside me—something I couldn't even reach. With her eyes, her voice, and the touch of her hand, she was telling me I was safe, and not to be afraid to tell her what was going on. "Whatever it is, Sol, I'll handle it. *We'll* handle it." She never said those words, but I could hear them. I wanted to hear them—I needed to.

I told her everything, and she listened. I told her we had no money. I apologized for failing her and our daughter. I said I didn't know what we were going to do. I promised to make things right. She listened to me, and I understood, many years later, that she heard everything she needed to hear. She heard that I was broken. She heard that I was scared. She heard that I was lost, confused, and insecure. She heard that I was hurting, angry, and wanted revenge.

I was trying to make her understand why I had gotten the knife, why I needed some sort of satisfaction for what I had suffered, when she interrupted me and said, "What did you learn working with Dan?" It was a question I didn't expect. I wasn't comfortable with it either. She was asking me to think well of Dan, to be beholden to him. "Tell me," she said. "What do you know about yourself now that you didn't know before you started that job?" She gave me time to think about it.

"I can sell," I said.

"Isn't that worth $18,000.00?" She took the knife and put it away. "That's what you take with you when you walk out that door."

Carol was my hero that day. She saw who I was, not just the man I was showing her. She also saw who I could be, and she was demanding that I let go of the old man I was so desperate to protect and embrace the new one. She had allowed God to give her the words to say to me. (What would I have paid to know what I had just learned about myself?) All my anger was gone suddenly, and I could breathe, only in a different way than I had before that day. I was like a baby who lives inside his mother's womb until the violence of birth thrusts him into a new home and, with a painful slap, forces him to herald his own arrival.

Babies don't have a choice. They cannot stop themselves from being born. Through no action on their part, their mother's bellies simply won't accommodate them anymore and they have to give it up and live a new way. We, on the other hand, always have a choice to be born into a better life, or to stay where we are. We can hold onto what's familiar to us, in the dark without sufficient space or resources to grow, or we can allow ourselves to be catapulted into the next adventure, sometimes painfully, but never fatally.

We can pretend we're strong, confident, and essential, and then demand that others agree, or we can actually become those things by understanding the truth that real power is always a partner to weakness not its opposite; that our specific assortment of frailties—the "junk" in our basements—is actually the peculiar treasure we carry through this world to uniquely bless everybody who crosses our path.

I never got the $18,000.00 from Dan. I never asked him for it. I saw him once more, and took it as an opportunity to go up to him and say, "Thank you for what you did for me."

I am grateful. Without him, I would never know what I was born to do.

Inner Space

Nothing can prevent me from succeeding. Some things have hurt me, scarred me, and caused me to change direction. Sometimes life isn't fair, and we find ourselves lost, confused, and insecure. But there's so much to learn in these places. I want to learn all the lessons my life has to teach me.

Read this paragraph a few times. What memories and feelings come up as you reflect on it?

Think and write about **1** habit, memory, or feeling you struggle to let to of, **2** things that give you joy, and **3** people or groups of people you wish you could help or heal.

One thing I struggle with is allowing myself to be me when I'm around others who are not like me. Sometimes I find myself going with the flow of my friends most times, instead of be the person that God has called me to be. ① I love being able to show my wife how much I love & appreciate her, by giving her things that she wants & desires. ② I also love helping people become who they want to become & who they know God has made them to be. The groups of people I wish I could help or heal would be ① Homeless men who have the drive to do better. ② Young men who are willing to change the paradigm for their family's Bloodline. ③ People over seas who need help like in Africa + indonesia + other third world countries.

CHAPTER FIVE

Choice

To do what is right and just is more acceptable to the LORD than sacrifice.

–SOLOMON (PROVERBS 21:3)

Where the needs of the world and your talents cross, there lies your vocation.

– ARISTOTLE

Failure is 100% preventable because 100% of its power comes from our choosing it.

–SOL HICKS

❧ ❧

"I can sell."

I remember the day that statement took root in my understanding. I sensed it instantly transforming me; affirming and encouraging, adhering to every motivation, shaping my curiosity, and sorting my options. It was like observing the time-lapse flowering of a plant or the movement of clouds. All my life I had been satisfied just to have enough money to sustain me and my family. After that season with Dan though, my perspective changed.

Yes, I needed a job. However, it also seemed to be true that there were jobs which needed *me*!

Poring over the classifieds—with different eyes now— became a pleasurable activity, one I anticipated rather than dreaded. Executive coach and author Richard Leider says every job search should be both an adventure, and an "in-venture." By that he means that in order for us to make good decisions, we should be able to say that what looks good "out there" matches up with what's good "in here," that is, inside us. I didn't have Mr. Lieder looking over my shoulder as I was marking up the *Chicago Daily News* want ads, but I was definitely searching for something that would give me more than money. If you will permit me the indulgence of an obvious pun, I knew I needed work that made dollars and *sense*.

One morning, I found what appeared to be a perfect fit. The Prudential Insurance Company was recruiting people through its new TAP initiative. TAP stood for Training Allowance Program. In an effort to attract minority agents (and ultimately the relatively untouched pool of minority consumers), Prudential was offering to pay its new hires a weekly base salary of $200.00 while they were being trained, whether or not they earned that in commissions. The thinking was that agents would focus and learn faster without the added pressure to meet basic financial needs. I really wanted another sales job. Moreover, my basic financial needs were piling up, so I appreciated the thinking that inspired TAP. I called for an interview.

Carol had to work on the morning of my meeting with the sales manager at Prudential's Chicago office, so I brought Cynthia with me to the appointment. As a rule, I don't think 5-year-olds make the best accessories when you're trying to distinguish yourself in a job interview, however, Cynthia proved to be a charming, well-behaved, adorable exception. The manager's questions to me were almost an afterthought. He was clearly more interested in coaxing smiles and a giggles out of my daughter who, I have to admit, was pretty darn cute that day. Cynthia had so captivated the man, that he hired me without knowing some key information. He didn't know that I didn't have a phone, or a car.

Let me put this in perspective for you. Employing a salesman with no phone or car in those days was like hiring a cabbie without a driver's license, a chef with no taste buds, or a drummer with no rhythm. It just was not done.

Carol and I didn't have a phone at home because we simply couldn't afford one. The day I got that job, we had exactly $6.00 in the bank. The month before that I had taken my car, a Satellite Plymouth with over 300,000 miles on it, to what we called an "alley mechanic" because I couldn't get it fixed at a regular shop. They wanted too much money up front. The man I left it with said he would do all the repairs necessary and that I could pay him in installments. I thought that was a great deal. A couple of weeks later, he told me to come get my car because it was "taking up space" in his garage. He neglected to tell me that he had been running it—during a Chicago winter—with no anti-freeze and had broken the engine block.

None of that mattered to me when I circled that Prudential ad in the paper. I had called from a phone booth for the interview and Cynthia and I had taken the bus to the office. I was sure I could do the job without a car or a home phone. Still, I wasn't naïve. I knew it would become a long shot once they knew my situation. That's why when the manager didn't ask about it, I didn't volunteer the information.

I started work the following week. Because of the bus schedule, I would get to the office about an hour and a half early and then wait for my boss to get there to unlock the door. He was very impressed since he was used to being the first one in. I made my calls in the morning from my desk at the office, and then took the bus to my afternoon and evening appointments.

This worked out well until I needed directions to a part of town that I wasn't familiar with. I asked one of the other agents where it was. He tried to give me driving directions, but I told him I would be on the bus. He questioned me further and I eventually confided my circumstances to him. I could tell he was shocked, and I asked him not to make an issue of it or tell our manager. He promised he wouldn't, but I saw the two of them talking shortly after that. When the boss turned to me and angrily ordered me into his office, I knew the promise had not been kept.

He fired me before I got the door closed. He called me a liar and accused me of deliberately deceiving him and taking advantage of him. I calmly told him that I had not lied to him, that I answered every question he had asked me truthfully. I didn't begrudge him his reaction. I understood why he was upset. No one from the Pru home office was going to ask me why I was crazy enough to take that job. Who wouldn't? I was guaranteed a salary whether I worked or not. They were going to ask him why he was crazy—or careless—enough to give it to me and then make them pay for his mistake.

He didn't want to hear anything I had to say. He let me have it, and when he was finished, he told me to get out, but I wouldn't go. I had decided to fight and I figured I didn't have anything to lose at that point trying to reason with him, since he was already furious.

I said I was sorry for not telling him about the phone and the car, and I appealed to his mind, ignoring his combustible emotions. I pointed out that the company already had to pay me for the week. Why not let me work? "If I don't perform, you can fire me," I said. He was still mad, but I could tell that what I had said made sense to him. He decided finally that he would let me work, but he wasn't going to make it easy. In fact, he seemed determined to make that the last week I worked at Prudential. He took away my desk, use of the office phone, and all my leads. I would be a "canvassing agent," which meant I would have to generate my own leads and use all my own resources. I had been expecting business cards, but was told that I wouldn't be getting those either.

There was a time not long before this when I wouldn't have asked to keep my job, especially after the way I had just been berated and humiliated. It would have made me feel like a beggar. You might think a person with just $6.00 in the bank should be willing to beg, and that might have been a consideration for me, but only a small one. I remember my thinking exactly during that awful exchange. It was very hard to take. Everyone in the office heard him yelling at me; calling me names and implying that I was too stupid to do the job I had obviously tricked him into giving me. The average guy (I considered myself one), wouldn't put up that regardless of his circumstances. However, more prominent in my thoughts than that was an absolute certainty that this man had no idea who I was. He had no idea how perfect this job was for me, and he would not know unless and until I proved it to him. What mattered most to me was getting that chance.

Selling for Dan I had begun to discover my gifts, and I was sure I was the right man for Prudential, so sure that I was willing to start at a disadvantage and work my way up. I knew that was a small price to pay for the opportunity to do what I believed I was designed to do.

I didn't know it then, but I had chosen the career that would take me through the next 36 years of my life. What's most important about that statement is not the career itself, or the more than three and a half decades I would spend in it. The most significant thing—and the key to making every wise decision—is that act of choosing. Whatever we do, especially when it comes to the work we do, until we choose it, as a conscious act of our will, it won't matter. That is, it won't matter to us, and if it doesn't matter to us, then we can't matter to it.

Leiber says, "Most people…didn't choose their career; their career chose them. They got into a line of work because they had to get a job, or somebody told them they'd be good at a job. They started down a certain path, and they never stopped to ask what their calling might be—not just their job, but their real calling. Then before they know it, they hit midlife, and they're asking themselves, 'Why am I doing this?'" To be clear, I think the real problem is not asking that question. The real problem is not being able to answer it, or having an answer that places responsibility on shoulders other than our own.

Wisdom is the willingness to make the choices which give you the freedom to be good and to do good for others. Choice, and the liberty inherent in the act, distinguishes wisdom from mere good advice or accurate information because it engages us in our own transformation and in the process of positively influencing others. That personal participation invests us in change at two levels.

First, conscious choice reinforces the truth that we contribute to our own success, and that setbacks never have to be permanent because we are empowered to make changes. Hard circumstances don't have to be a sentence imposed on us, but rather a season we can endure and decide to work out for our own good or the good of others.

My first weeks at Prudential were less than stellar. I used business cards that belonged to another agent. I scratched out his name and wrote my own. I made my calls from a phone booth in the parking lot of the Walgreen's Department Store. My leads were generated from the phone book. The bus took me to all my appointments. It was tantamount to starting a race from the bleachers, but I was the happiest I had ever been on any job. I went after it, got it, held onto it, and it was mine to lose or make remarkable.

Second, knowing that our choices influence change keeps us in a giving posture or one that focuses on what we have to offer. The ironic benefit of this mindset is an awareness that we are "filled" by the knowledge that we are valuable, because we have something of value to give. All gifts assume a giver. When we actively partake in our work, we acknowledge that we are both a gift and a generous giver.

I learned early on why selling insurance was such a fit for me. It wasn't the selling. I wasn't actually that good at persuading people. I was like the prophet Moses. I got tongue-tied and I didn't always use the right words to say what I wanted to say. It took me awhile to understand how to compute insurance rates, and I carried a pocket-sized chart around with me, referring to it often during presentations. In fact my first sale was to a man who appreciated my honesty in confessing that I didn't know how to compute his rate since his age was not on my card. "Are you sure you're not younger?" I joked before admitting

I would have to call him later with the rate.

True salesmen are glib and you can't always tell if they're stuck or don't know something since they're so good at covering their mistakes. I'm not that guy, and I probably wouldn't be even if I could. I do appreciate that kind of sharpness and I've seen it serve many people well. I was just never ashamed to admit what I didn't know. That's because while my vocation is sales, my skill isn't selling. My skill is with people. My gift isn't convincing people to do what they or may not want to do. It's building people up; by evaluating and explaining their needs, comforting them emotionally and spiritually, and then helping them make the decisions which adjust for past mistakes and bring a good future into better focus. Life insurance and financial planning lets me do all of that.

I went after the work I do because it suited me, but I enjoy it and feel empowered in it, even when it's hard and unfruitful, because I *chose* it. We can do many things, even to the satisfaction of others and with some success, without actually choosing them. Have you ever had a job—maybe you're currently in one—that you saw as "just a paycheck" or something "for now"? It's draining isn't it? Even an easy job depletes you if you don't see it as a choice you made for your life. But the moment you see and appreciate that you're in it because you chose to be, for whatever reason, you can begin to allow yourself to pour into it from the coffers of who you are. Then "for now" becomes a promise rather than a punishment, and your paycheck is not some huge, indispensable thing, but it's instead the thing that helps sustain your infinitely valuable existence.

Dr. Robert Schuller is fond of asking "What would you do if you knew that you could not fail?" I want to suggest to you that choosing eliminates the option of failing. Do I mean that you will never have setbacks? Of course I don't mean that. Will you suffer or do battle in some seasons? I expect you will. In fact, I hope you will, because pain and healing, hope and asking for help are all necessary for a good and productive life. None of those things equals failure.

Failure is no more than a conscious choice to quit choosing wisely when there are still choices to be made. Failure is retreat. It means I disengage and stop contributing myself to something or someone which can still benefit from what I can offer. Failure is not a prospect telling you no, learning that you're not good at something, getting fired, losing an account, struggling, or not scoring as many points as your competition. It's not being unappealing or unattractive to others. It isn't even a grown-up son or daughter who hates you, as painful as that is.

Real failure never happens *to* us or apart from our control. That's a frightening statement if we don't look too hard at it. If we keep those words on the surface of our thoughts, we'll only conclude that failure is our fault. It is. It always is. But sit with that for a moment. Sink into it and a deeper truth will meet you.

FAILURE is 100% preventable because 100% of its power comes from our choosing it.

I was without support when I started at Prudential, but I was never without options. As long as there were choices to make, I was going to make them. I didn't always like the ones open to me, but I could be certain of one thing. Among my options, there was always at least one wise choice, one choice that would give me the freedom to be good or do something good for someone else.

I chose to fight for my job instead of retreat. I wouldn't be given any customer leads, so I chose to offer life insurance and financial planning to the people in the phone book, in the Walgreen's parking lot, on the bus and at the bus stop. I didn't have a manager who wanted to coach me, so I chose to read the books that were lying around the office. I practiced my sales techniques out on my wife and in front of the bathroom mirror. I opted to ask the prospects who said no to me what I could do to improve my presentation. I chose to learn more about the products and services I was selling so I could better educate my clients, and came to believe in them even more.

Sometimes our instincts tell us that giving up or retreating is healthy and necessary for our self-esteem and our emotional wellbeing, as in the case with abuse or oppression. I don't disagree with that. Abuse is never a good place to dwell. But in reality, that's not retreat or giving up. It's moving forward. It's choosing to heal because continuing would not be good for you or the people connected to you. That is far from failure. That is freedom. The important thing is to know the difference between that and giving in to avoid leaving your comfort zone.

In those early days, I didn't have much of a comfort zone. I made many of my sales as a result of efforts to make the most of challenging circumstances. Because I was riding the bus, it took a long time to get to some of my appointments. If a client was very late, or stood me up altogether after I had spent an hour, sometimes two, riding across town to meet with them, the whole day was pretty much gone by the time I made it back to the office. After that happened a few times, I decided to be more efficient with my time, and hopefully more effective.

A prospect was no longer defined only as a man or woman I had scheduled an appointment with. It was expanded to include anyone I encountered on the way to or from that meeting.

Early one morning, I showed up for a scheduled meeting, and no one was home, so I approached a guy who was apparently just getting home from the previous night's activities. He didn't want to hear about any insurance. He was trying to figure out what excuse he could give his wife for being out all night. I asked him if he'd like me to go upstairs with him. I was thinking his wife might be less likely to make a scene with company around. (The relief on his face told me he was thinking she'd be less likely to hurt him in the presence of a witness!) When we got to his apartment, he introduced me to his wife and disappeared into one of the bedrooms.

She was fuming, waiting for me to handle my business with her husband so I could leave and she could handle hers. We waited, but he never came back. After a few minutes, she checked on him and informed me that he had gone to bed and was sound asleep. That was my cue to leave.

"Has he done this before?" I asked. She said he had. "Well, don't you think you should get some life insurance on him in case something happens while he's out there?" I don't know if that guy ever stayed out all night again, but his wife faithfully paid the premium on his policy.

Despite its shaky beginning, my first year at Prudential ended with me being named Rookie of the Year. Carol and I had a phone and a car again, and a little savings. I left the house every morning excited, and returned each evening grateful, and that didn't change if I had a bad day or a fight with my wife. It didn't change if I was unhappy or hit a slump. I couldn't have articulated it then, but I had discovered the paradoxical truth that pouring out fills us to overflowing, and that we can only know how valuable we are when we choose to add value to the world.

The Cabrini-Green housing projects on Chicago's North Side didn't see many salesmen. The crime and drug infested complex was a well-known gang haven, and the facility was so poorly neglected by the city that the stench of garbage piled several stories high could be smelled from blocks away. Its name eventually became synonymous with all that was wrong with public housing in the United States.

I didn't know all of that when I scheduled an appointment to discuss life insurance with a woman whose name I dialed at random from a phone book. When they learned where I was going, all of the agents in the office said I should not go meet this woman alone, but none of them would go with me, and many of them suggested I just cancel. But I thought this family needed something I could give them, and I didn't know what else mattered more than that. People died every day all over Chicago. This was what I was made for, wasn't it?

Canceling the appointment was out of the question. I arrived there in the evening and immediately understood why no one wanted to come to Cabrini-Green…and then quickly concluded that's why I had to. The woman I went to see lived on the fourth floor, but the graffiti-covered elevator wasn't operating, so I went to the stairwell. There were no working lights in the hallways, so I felt my way up, stepping on and over trash and bottles. Once or twice I heard the scurrying of living things in the dark, but I didn't stop to find out what they were.

She was there with her husband and two children. I sat down with her and we talked. She told me she didn't expect me to keep the appointment. She had been trying for years to get someone out to talk about insurance, but once agents found out where she lived, they mysteriously lost interest in her business. She made my gesture sound grander than it was and I was actually a little embarrassed about the discussions that had taken place at my office earlier, but I was glad I was there. I wrote a policy for her and spent a little more time socializing before I left. I practically ran down the stairs, not in fear, but because I was thrilled to be able to help this woman who had waited so long for someone to care enough to act on her behalf.

Less than six months later, her husband, on his way home from work, was robbed and beaten to death with a steel pipe...right outside the Cabrini-Green projects.

I personally delivered her settlement payment. The wife I had talked to just months earlier was now a widow answering the door and offering me the same gentle hospitality she had before. "God sent you to me," she said flatly as she looked at the check I handed to her. There was nothing dramatic about her declaration. It was just the communication of a fact that struck her, so she shared it.

For me it was a defining moment, a simple but powerful revelation of the true value of what I was called to do for people. This was the first work I had ever chosen; the first time I had a job not just for what it could give to me, but for what I could give to it. I was designed for this by God, and His work is never designed to fail, so I could not fail at it unless I chose not to succeed at it.

My thoughts were suspended then affirmed by the sight of the woman's two now fatherless children. They could never be compensated for what they had just lost, but they would not go hungry. Their mother could move if she wanted to. Maybe one day, they would go to college. They could, without worries, because their parents loved them enough to secure that for them…and I had played a small part in that. Wow.

I let my imagination carry me again, back to that first night I had come to Cabrini-Green. I remembered, as I felt my way up the stairs, a thought I had. "No light. What a horrible way for people to live, without lights."

That day I chose to devote myself to helping people find their way.

Inner Space

Success is mine if I choose it. I contribute to it by participating in my own development and empowerment. I'm better at some things than others. There are some things I notice before others do, some pain that I understand better because it's personal to me. I'm uniquely formed by my experiences and my environment. That means I can uniquely transform whatever situation or circumstance I encounter. I will choose not to fail.

Read this paragraph a few times. What experiences, encounters, or feelings come up as you reflect on the validity of it?

Think and write about **1** gift you'd like to develop more, **2** decisions you're glad you made, and **3** people or processes you'd like to be able to influence.

I'D like to become more of a people person + be able to hold warm chatter with people who I don't Know. Two decision that I'm glad I made is ① Rededicating my life back to God when I was 20yrs. old + a Sophmore in College. ② I'm also glad That I chose to get married + start building my life together with my wife at an early age. I'd like to be able to influence

My 2 sisters Bernadette & Cynthia & her husband Larry that they deserve to live a better life than our parents lived. ② The second Group of people I would love to influence is my parents + my wife's parents, as well as the black community in America. I say this group, because I often feel as if this group is so influenced by their environment & by the things talked about in this chapter, that I know God has charted another course for me to take, not Just for me, but for others as well. ③ The last process would be the economy. I feel that God has given me vision that will be able to have an effect on our economy, & I welcome the idea of knowing that God has entrusted me with that assignment.

CHAPTER SIX

Counting The Cost

Finish your outdoor work and get your fields ready; after that, build your house.

—SOLOMON (PROVERBS 24:27)

In this world it is not what we take up, but what we give up, that makes us rich.

— HENRY WARD BEECHER

My thinking was as long as I served people, I would be successful... I had been blessed with so many teachers. Now I was in a position to teach, guide, and offer what I knew to others.

—SOL HICKS

ॐ ☙

Someone said once that half of knowing what you want is found in knowing what you've got to give up before you can get it.

Get that, and you can face anything. In fact, you'll charge the darkness if you think your destiny is on the other side of it, once you know that however it comes, discomfort is not a sentence imposed on you, but rather an invitation to grow. Wisdom requires that we make decisions to navigate our way through necessary pain as much as around unnecessary pain.

Wanting more out of life isn't a bad thing. Contentment doesn't preclude change, increase, or the shedding of unnecessary baggage. But you don't get stronger without heavy lifting. Patience isn't produced apart from waiting. Salvation is for the imperiled and the lost. Healing only follows hurting. Gratitude for friends, wealth, or promotion is inextricably attached to an understanding of loneliness, poverty, and the pain of being overlooked. Hardship is a feature of most worthwhile pursuits, but if we endure, it's always constructive and ultimately beneficial.

Even before my job at the Drive 'Round It, I was acquainted with hard work. I helped our milkman Mr. Blackmon with his deliveries. I would ride on the back of his truck. When we passed a house he needed to service, Mr. Blackmon would slow down and I'd jump off with the required bottles of milk or other dairy. I had to be fast— make my delivery and pick up any empty bottles—because Mr. Blackmon only slowed down. He didn't stop his truck from the beginning of his route until the end unless he absolutely had to. I didn't make much working for Mr. Blackmon, but what the job lacked in salary and a health plan (for the occasional scraped knee), it more than made up for in fun.

Back then, I didn't know how to spell entrepreneur, but I was one. Along the side of the roads in Eufaula, blackberries grew wild and plentifully. In addition to working for Mr. Blackmon, when I had time, I would pick them—about three or four quarts worth at a time—and sell them door-to-door for 50 cents a quart. Just before I knocked, I would arm myself with the very biggest smile I could stretch across my 7-year-old face. A typical conversation would go something like this:

"Would you like to buy some blackberries, Mrs. So-and-so?"

"Solomon, I just bought some of those berries from you yesterday!"

"Well, what did you do with them?"

"I made a pie."

"Was it good? Because if it was good, it's probably almost gone, and you're gonna need some more blackberries to make another one, aren't you? Or if you don't want to do that, think of all the other things you might make?"

I did all right for a 7-year-old, and I had heard my grandfather talk often about saving money, so I always made sure to put a little of what I earned away.

"Are you saving your money, boy?" he asked me one day.

"Yeah, Pop." I was proud to have the right answer for him.

"Does it hurt?"

"No, Pop." I thought he'd be glad that it wasn't hard for me to do the right thing, but he surprised me.

"Aw, then you ain't doin' nothin' boy." He saw my confusion and added, "Anything worth having is worth making a sacrifice for. You should save enough for it to hurt you."

Granddad's words came back to me many years later working at the bank in Chicago. Mr. Levine was one of our best customers. He came in often and greeted everyone including me. I was always impressed by him. He wore a nice hat and coat, and most times there was a cigar trapped between his teeth or resting in the crook of his forefinger as he conducted his business. He seemed to know that he was important, but wasn't particularly interested in informing others of that fact. I knew that he had money, but unlike some of our other clients, Mr. Levine appeared to be very skilled at holding onto his.

I approached him eventually and asked him if he would teach me what he knew. I wanted to be successful like him. He brightened immediately. Clearly he had been waiting for somebody to flip on the switch of his specific offering and he was ready with his response.

After that day, whenever Mr. Levine came into the bank, he made it a point to stop by my window and show me something. "Most people," he would say, "just want to have wealth, but they don't want to make sacrifices." My grandfather's words were in my head again. *Does it hurt, boy? If it don't hurt, then you ain't doin' nothin'.*

The first thing Mr. Levine taught me was how to "live off the 80." He gave the first 10 percent of everything he earned to God, and then he saved the next 10 percent. He lived on the 80 percent that was left. He talked about investing, and planning for retirement. I knew how to compute the time it would take to accumulate a specific amount of money and how long it would take to double that amount. By the time I had met and proposed to Carol, I had already put many of the principles I learned into practice. Mr. Levine is the reason I felt confident enough to promise her a secure future.

Author and sales guru Brian Tracy says, "No one lives long enough to learn everything they need to learn starting from scratch. To be successful, we absolutely, positively have to find people who have already paid the price to learn the things that we need to learn to achieve our goals." Pop had planted something in me that Mr. Levine built upon which both of them had learned from experience. If you had asked me what that was when I was 20, I would have said just that they taught me how to make sacrifices for what I wanted. I was much older before I drank really deeply from the well that these two great men had put in my path.

Where It Hurts

When I joined Prudential, I thought I could change the world. This company, I decided, was in the business of giving light. Life insurance, investments, savings, financial planning and disability insurance were all ways to shed light on the future and make it less frightening to people.

When I helped parents set money aside for their kids to go to college, it gave those children light. When people saved or invested their money, or insured a loved one, it was because I had helped them see the path to security. For me, being a light was being a servant. Think about it. Light is always there to help others. My thinking was as long as I served people, I would be successful, and I knew I was serving them if they could see the wonderful things I was trying to show them. The same way I had gotten help throughout my life, I wanted to give it. I had been blessed with so many teachers. Now I was in a position to teach, guide, and offer what I knew to others.

I was successful at work. I loved what I was doing, and people responded to me. At home, Carol was a constant source of encouragement and counsel. My kids—we had two daughters now—waited for me to come home so they could help me send out letters to my clients. They licked stamps, and folded notices. I paid them in nickels and chewing gum, and taught them how to save the way my grandfather and Mr. Levine had taught me.

Besides work and home, there was God, but despite my mother's admonitions and prayers to the contrary, I didn't see the need to pursue anything other than a casual acknowledgement of His existence "up there."

I didn't exactly avoid religion, but there was something about the absolute dependence on God which my mother advocated that just didn't sit well with me.

Growing up, I don't remember a time when God was not a part of my mother's vocabulary, experience, or instruction. He was like an invisible boarder, a kind of King-in-residence. He had a say in every major decision that was made. Sometimes it was the only say. Mom talked to Him before she talked to anybody. As we became adults, my sisters followed her example. I guess I preferred to be the one responsible for all the things that mattered to me. If God wanted to help me out—on my terms, of course—He was more than welcome. They seemed to need Him, but I was different, I thought. I had no real complaints, worries, or needs. Work was good. Home was good. I was good. Nothing essential appeared to be missing.

Does it hurt, boy? No Pop.

I had managed to stand on the outskirts of zealous faith without too much effort, and I planned to continue on that way...until I was presented with a rather dramatic alternative.

I was visiting my sister Bea in the hospital where she was being treated for Stevens-Johnson syndrome (SJS), a severe and adverse allergic reaction to drugs, chemicals, or medication. On the tame end of the spectrum, SJS is characterized by a rash on the skin and mucous membranes. Bea's "rash" was at the other extreme. Her skin was erupting, on the surface and underneath in lesions and blisters. Patients literally burn from the inside out because the pores can scar shut, causing them to retain heat. Bea's eyes had stopped producing tears and her lashes had begun to grow inward scratching her tender eyeballs. Every 20 minutes she was given drops to moisten and relieve her eyes.

Bea had been working on her doctorate at Fisk University. She was doing some laboratory research with various toxic substances. No one knew that the vents had been shut off in the lab and Bea was first exposed to the dangerous chemicals, and then had an allergic reaction to the medication she was given. She had withered to 100 pounds and her skin peeled away at the touch. The family took turns in the room with her, talking, listening, or getting whatever she needed.

Her doctors had given up and were treating Bea more for comfort than cure. Fortunately I didn't come from a family who knew when to say quit. My sister Dorothy was praying and came to the hospital with a tape recorder, which she put under Bea's bed. On it were healing scriptures. "We've heard the doctors. Let's see what Jesus can do," she said. Bea had lost her hair, and after Dot's "prescription" it began to grow back.

Normally, my sisters could count on me for some encouragement, but this scared me. I didn't want to see her. I tried to send Carol to check on her, but she refused. She loved my sisters, and she knew that Bea was specifically asking to see me.

When I got up the nerve to go and see her, I have to say, I was glad for a moment that she couldn't see. My heart was broken and I'm sure I didn't hide it. I could only do what brothers do, make awkward conversation, fetch things, and give comfort when the need arose. My mom and sisters would pray with her, but I wasn't comfortable doing that, and thankfully Bea didn't insist.

On this particular day, I was sitting in the room doing nothing special really. All errands had been run. The nurses and doctors had been in and had done their work. Breakfast and lunch had been eaten and all dishes and trays had been bussed to their proper locations. I was keeping an eye on very little in the tiny sterile room that was finally quiet for a change, when Bea, who I had assumed was sleeping, said softly, "Read to me, brother."

That was simple enough. I went downstairs to the gift shop and bought a few magazines. I returned shortly, pulled a chair up next to her bed and started reading aloud from *People* magazine. A paragraph or two into an article I don't remember now, about some star I have also forgotten, my sister stopped me. The voice was still soft but certain this time. "No, not that. Read me the Bible, Chuck." It was next to her bed, and I looked at it a moment before I picked it up.

"What do you want me to read in there?" It was a halfhearted attempt to be accommodating. The Bible was the last thing I wanted to look at.

"Read me the four gospels," she said meekly, dissolving any kernel of a scheme I had to circumnavigate her request. More than anything I wanted to please her. I wished I could take away her pain, but since I couldn't, I would do whatever made it easier to endure.

I turned to the index. It should be here, I was thinking. My sister read the Bible a lot, so I didn't imagine she'd ask me to look up something and give me the wrong name for it. The silence was starting to make me a little uncomfortable. Finally, Bea's voice put an end to it. "Chuck?"

"I'm looking, Bea. There's no book called "Four Gospels" anywhere in here."

My sister. She was so kind and careful with her answer that my own ignorance never even occurred to me. She seemed to be correcting herself when she told me she wanted me to read from Matthew, Mark, Luke, and John. I saw those names in the index right away, and I was happy to turn to them and start reading.

At some point—I don't know when—I began to hear the sound of my own voice, and then actually pay attention to it. A lot of what I was reading wasn't making sense to me, so I'd stop and ask Bea to explain it. She knew so much about genealogies, Jewish culture, Matthew, Mark, Luke, and John and their intentions when they authored the books. The more she taught me, the more I wanted to know, and somewhere along the way, we switched places. She was doing most of the talking, and I was the one listening.

Like Granddad and Mr. Levine, my sister had begun to teach me something I was suddenly desperate to know. We moved seamlessly from the academic to the personal, from information to significance. I wanted to know about Jesus.

Before that day, He didn't occupy much of my interest, much less my curiosity. I had been told often that He "so loved the world." In that moment, I needed to know if He loved *me*. He saved the world, but would He save *me*? Did He want *me*?

I felt like my life depended on everything Bea was telling me. We both forgot which one of us was the patient. She had become the physician, there to heal and reassure me. She was amazing! Then, just as I grasped the wonder of what was happening, Bea let out a loud scream followed by more screams. I was stunned momentarily until I saw that she was raising her hands the way I had seen her raise them when she was praying or singing hymns. She was rejoicing, for me, and those screams were the evidence that her tearless eyes couldn't give me. She was crying, for me…for *me*.

I got it. Christ was willing to suffer because He loved this world His Father had made and the people in it. Now He was showing me that same love through my sister who didn't let pain stop her from telling me what I needed to know. *Anything worth having is worth making a sacrifice for. I got it. Thanks Pop. Thank you, Mr. Levine. Thank you Bea.* I got it.

But I had still only gotten a part of it.

You see, sacrifice is an interesting picture but most of us only see one half of it. We usually just take note of the part where we have to give up some possession, where it costs us what we have in money, time, potency, calm, or security.

I suspect that the average person doesn't really take issue with the idea of giving sacrificially. Most of us care sufficiently enough about at least one person or thing to relinquish something for them or it. But you see that's just one side of sacrifice; the *attractive* side, the side we're more comfortable with.

Forfeiting stuff—no matter the value of the stuff—is not so hard a thing to understand. Granted, we feel a loss, maybe even a great one, but we're never confused about what it is that we're doing. For the most part, we are okay with the notion of giving up what we have for what we want. What we're not okay with is the deeper cost that truly complete sacrifice seeks to exact. At the end of the day, sacrifice is not just asking us for what we have. It's also after *who we are*. Learning the difference can be painful. Not learning it can be devastating.

The Sunday following my life-changing experience with

Bea, I took my family to church and formally committed myself to Jesus, to serving Him and knowing Him the way my mom and sisters did.

Let me tell you, I had no idea what that looked like. I couldn't imagine that the guy I saw in the mirror every morning could ever be as spiritually certain, as powerful, or as confident as those women and some of the devout men I had met in my life. They were "there" and I was solidly "here." The space between us stretched further than I could see or imagine.

But I had read somewhere in the Bible I was now greedily consuming, that faith assumes the unimaginable. Even from where I was, it said, God would build bridges to promises I could only ache for, because they were beyond my mind's ability to give them shape. He could set my feet upon them even before I had taken a first step. If I trusted Him to be who He said He was, I would find out, one day at a time, what the basketball player in the Adidas ads knows that drives him to deny gravity its just wages and walk on the sky: Impossible is nothing.

I decided that a life which gave me more than my imagination was worth all I could think of giving up. Then I discovered that Impossible doesn't come quite so cheaply.

Inner Space

My purpose on earth is to succeed. Nothing that important comes without sacrifice. I won't get stronger without heavy lifting. Patience only comes with waiting. Healing only follows hurt, and support is only for those who admit that they don't have all the power or all the answers. The greatest treasure is always hidden from the slacker and the coward. I want the irrevocable rewards of humility, endurance, and courage.

Read this paragraph a few times. What thoughts, people, or feelings come up as you reflect on the challenges in it?

Think and write about **1** person/thing you have made a sacrifice for, **2** changes you can make to improve your life, and **3** people who could profit from an hour of your undivided attention.

I know that my life is designed to succeed in everything that God has ordained for me to succeed in. The issue that I sometimes wrestle with is being able to bring out (better yet) let my self birth out what God has planted inside of me. I want God to be pleased with my life, I want God to be pleased with me. I really don't ever want to miss the move of God in my life. But, I also know that there is a process that must take place before every promise

is released. ① I think I have made a sacrifice
to be my Age, + be married, have a house,
+ be involved in leadership at my church. I had to
sacrifice a lot of things that most young men at 23
would not be willing to give up to be where I am.
② Changes I can make to improve my life would be
Spend more personal time with God. ⑤ Spend more
time alone + getting to know more about me +
how I function + operate. ③ People who could
benefit from an hour in my presence. Joshua
Warren my younger Brother, Judan Ellington
a friend of my wife, Ronald Hunter Jr.
My brother in law.

CHAPTER SEVEN

In The Dark

The lamp of the LORD searches the spirit of a man; it searches out his inmost being.

—SOLOMON (PROVERBS 20:27)

Believe, when you are most unhappy, that there is something for you to do in the world.

— HELLEN KELLER

Frying pan or fire, the heat is there to teach us something new about our strength, our power, the actual depth of our joy, the effectiveness of prayers, faith, integrity, and vision.

—SOL HICKS

∂◦ ◦∫

Reverend Milton Brunson was a dynamic preacher and a devoted pastor. Attending his church fed me in ways that affirmed and encouraged the new direction my life was taking. He talked about Jesus in practical, active terms. He wasn't just high, wide, and far reaching. He was also close, enabling, and trustworthy and I needed that. I needed to know that the same Savior, who had entered my sister's hospital room and miraculously restored her health, could be with me in the unspectacular. I had a family to love and take care of. I wanted to follow a Jesus who cared if my daughter was hungry and agreed with me that my wife was beautiful. I wanted Him to show me how to do my job well.

At Rev. Brunson's church, I learned that success was not an unreligious ideal, but rather a holy command that all creation was designed to obey as it followed God. I cut my teeth on scriptures like John 10:10. He came, Rev. Brunson explained, so that we could have a great, more than sufficient, overflowing, better than wonderful life. "Abundant life," he said, went beyond God helping us do the things that matter to us. It meant that He would deepen our desires to match His own depth of concern. He would give us a burden to make a difference, then transform that burden into a vision, and give us the courage and power to walk in that vision.

Living life abundantly meant discovering and using my God-given talents and abilities to help others. Nothing that ever happens to us is wasted. Rev. Brunson taught me that my entire life had reason. Every moment of it was valuable in the economy of God, even if I couldn't see it, but that some things would be revealed if I simply began to use my spiritual eyes. Some things were waiting for me alone. They would only reveal themselves to my unique understanding and experience. There were some questions in the world that were calling out to answers that God had planted specifically inside me. I began to ask Him in prayer what they were.

Soon I became acutely aware of so much financial oppression around me. Families were struggling to live sufficiently on more than adequate incomes. Husbands would die and I would somehow learn that they had left their widows and children with nothing. Children had stopped dreaming of college and focused their attention on helping to meet immediate needs at home. I saw beautiful cars in the parking lot that belonged to people whose homes were being foreclosed on and fur coats on the backs of women who had no heat in their apartments.

Every Sunday, we would sing praises to God who "owned the cattle on a thousand hills." Our pastor would preach over and over from Deuteronomy 28:12, 13:

> *The Lord shall open unto thee his good treasure, the heaven to give the rain unto thy land in his season, and to bless all the work of thine hand: and thou shalt lend unto many nations, and thou shalt not borrow. And the Lord shall make thee the head, and not the tail; and thou shalt be above only, and thou shalt not be beneath...*

I repeated that passage to myself. I hid it in my heart and believed it. Then I would look around me, and suddenly I was alone. It was as if the good treasure of God was being put into pockets with holes in them. The promised rain seemed to evaporate before it ever reached a seed. So many were borrowing; few were lending.

The reality of so much financial bondage weighed my soul down and I prayed, as much for my own relief as I did for solutions. My heart was hurting for these people who couldn't see past today. I was afraid for their children who would have nothing but a legacy of debt, lack, and poverty to give their own offspring.

I was also grateful for my own upbringing. I had a grandfather who taught me about saving. My mother was never wasteful. Miss Solita let me look over her shoulder as she did her accounting and made time for dreaming about owning my own restaurant one day. Dr. McCoo was a generous man, and showed me that the purpose for having anything was found in giving to others. All of their wisdom had been woven into the fabric of my thinking and behavior. Even when Carol and I were struggling, it never occurred to me to settle there as if "poor" was an actual arriving point. Somewhere in my living, I had come to believe that it was never more than a point of pivot before a change in direction. God had shaped my insides long before I knew Him.

I decided to take God and Rev. Brunson at their word, and make it my business to understand the promises in Deuteronomy 28. I began to study it on my own and pray for clarity. It came quickly, at the end of the passage, a part that doesn't often get preached.

> *The Lord shall open unto thee his good treasure, the heaven to give the rain unto thy land in his season, and to bless all the work of thine hand: and thou shalt lend unto many nations, and thou shalt not borrow. And the Lord shall make thee the head, and not the tail; and thou shalt be above only, and thou shalt not be beneath; if that thou hearken unto the commandments of the Lord thy God, which I command thee this day, to observe and do them.*

The promises to Israel in this passage—and by extension to us—were conditional. They required our participation through obedience. We were commanded to love our neighbors, protect the helpless, be holy, merciful, forgiving, and patient, just, and raise knowledgeable and honoring children. Financially, we were commanded to give to the poor, be good stewards of what we have, save for the future, stay out of debt, and not be greedy or selfish.

Obedience assumes an authority, and an instruction... and often an *instructor*. Looking at my burden with new eyes, I saw what I had not seen before. The people were not choosing to subjugate themselves to debt and destructive financial habits without help. All around me I saw that teachers, elders, and deacons—the influencers in our ministry—were some of the most flagrant offenders. People were hopeless in life and dying in poverty in part because their leaders were not practicing what they were preaching.

"My people are destroyed for a lack of knowledge."

It was a verse I had been drawn to often. Now it had practical significance. Leaders lead. If I was ever going to see my burden lifted and witness people experience the kind of liberation I knew was possible, I was going to have to start at the top.

Like a laser, the burden in me drew my attention to pastors and other ministry heads. I went first to Rev. Brunson and shared what I knew with him. He listened intently as I talked to him about what was troubling me. I talked about what was in my spirit concerning good stewardship, and how the people would follow if the leaders would lead them in a right direction. I told him how Mr. Levine had taught me about paying yourself first, living on 80% of your income, and "the rule of 72" which would help a person compute how long it would take to double any amount of savings. I volunteered to teach him, his friends, and our congregation everything I knew. I was thrilled when he agreed that it was a great idea.

I was introduced to our church leadership as well as pastors of churches in the area, and many of them purchased insurance policies from me. They took the time to listen to what I had to say to them about guiding people by the example of their own journey to financial freedom. That intersection of spiritual and secular work was sweet to me and I settled into it with ease.

There's a lot to be said for discovering your purpose. When I look at the lives of people I would say live or have lived successfully, what becomes obvious is that at given moments, something in them—something that is inseparable *from* them—appears at the surface of who they are. The same way you see the chest of a man rise and fall with his breathing, you see his God-given power when he's in his God-given groove; that activity, gift, cause, or function that gives him a shine. He seems made for it, and it for him.

What would you do if no one paid you? What calls out from inside you that your experience and surroundings conspired to place in you? What feels life-giving to you and seems life-giving when you offer it to others? For me it is the ideal of wise stewardship. How we take care of whatever treasure we have matters to me more than the average person. It's not just a financial issue either. It's also relational, spiritual, physical, emotional, and environmental. I tend to look at all things through a lens of stewardship and it excites me when others see what I see.

The announcement was made at church the following Sunday that the congregation shouldn't miss the next week's service, because they would be learning "how to double their money." It was a catchy way to promote what I was doing. It was very effective too. On the morning I was to speak, the pews were packed with eager souls anxious, I thought, to receive the pearls that had encouraged, guided, and transformed me. I was all geared up to pour out everything I believed God had given me to say.

I was nervous at first and it showed. I was no Rev. Brunson. Still, my audience was polite. However, after about ten minutes or so, it was apparent that they were waiting for me to give them "the formula" for doubling their money. They didn't seem to want to be kept waiting, so I hastened to my main points. I recounted all the lessons of my life. I told them about saving, investing, leaving an inheritance for their children's children like the wise man in the Bible. I talked about going without for a better return down the road, sacrificial giving, and budgeting, setting goals and sticking to them even when it hurts. Granddad, Mr. Levine, mom, Miss Solita and the rest would've been proud, I thought.

I was giving them the tools to turn their circumstances around. As one writer put it, "if you want a miracle you first need to do whatever it is you can do—if that's to plant, then plant; if it is to read, then read; if it is to change, then change; if it is to study, then study; if it is to work, then work; whatever you have to do. And then you will be well on your way to doing the labor that works miracles."

I was doing what I needed to. I was teaching them what I had been taught. Plus, I had just joined Prudential, and I shared what I was still learning, certain that the only thing these good people were missing was practical information about how to handle their money.

Then, one by one, men and women raised polite fingers and tiptoed out of the service. They were not interested in anything practical. They wanted to reap a harvest that would magically appear, without rain, and without planting or plowing. Since I wasn't showing them how to do that, they would be on their way to Sunday brunch. By the time I finished, the church and the parking lot were almost empty.

My attempts to help were flatly rejected. No one even thanked me for the effort. Pastor Brunson returned to the pulpit the following weeks and so did his flock. It was as if I had never been there. Adding to my frustration was the fact that many of the pastors I had written business for were not paying their premiums. Eventually many of their policies lapsed and the calls I made to rectify the situation weren't returned. Every image I had of commitment and integrity was being challenged by the very men and women charged with holding up those ideals.

It would be a great lie to say that I handled my disappointment in the church with grace; that I saw my less-than-stellar venture into ministry as an opportunity to grow. The truth is I was angry and hurt. I was sure that what I believed was still true. People were struggling in debt and their shepherds weren't rushing to help them. However, I concluded their troubles weren't my problem anymore. I had done my part. I couldn't make them do theirs.

I decided to turn my anger into action. If they wouldn't listen, I would find others who would. I returned all of my attention to non-ministry related business. My recent experience made me determined and fixated. I was zealous to prove out in the world that I was exceptional and talented, and worthier than I had been given credit for being in the church.

Good was no longer good enough. I had to be great. I didn't want to be knowledgeable or informed, but *expert*. Improvement only mattered if it meant winning, and winning was nice, but I wanted to be untouchable; number one with number two invisible behind me.

This was my drive. I convinced myself that I was making every sacrifice to do what God had designed me to do, and that if I became the best at it, every yearning inside me would be met, every void filled. I was certain that the lack of peace gnawing on my insides would be eased when I became "Number One," so that was the object I set before me.

I was unstoppable. I gave myself to the business of selling life insurance. I woke up early and stayed up late. My wife kept records and my children licked stamps on the mailers I sent out. I devoured every book on leadership, sales, and business I could get my hands on. I read up on all the products Prudential offered, and knew how they compared to our competitors' services. If there was an edge to be had, I had it.

My efforts were rewarded with the recognition and approval of my peers. Even the company's executives were taking notice. I was invited to speak at conferences. As one of only a few African American agents excelling, I got calls from all over the country to advise and motivate individuals and I became a fixture at many of Prudential's diversity-focused meetings. Sales managers who met me at different gatherings asked me to come out and inspire their teams.

One of those trips took me to Southern California. I had met a particularly enthusiastic manager at our yearly conference in Hawaii. He told me how impressed he was with my performance and he marveled at what I had been able to accomplish in my career. He had heard me speak and always liked what I had to say, and wondered if I could stop by his agency on my way back to Chicago and talk to his sales force.

This was not an unusual request, and I was happy to honor it, being a very different man from the one who had disgraced Rev. Brunson's platform years earlier. No one would politely walk out and I didn't expect them to, confident that I had something to say and that there were people who wanted to hear it. The following Friday morning, I addressed his agency.

Afterwards, it felt good to have my ego stroked by this California manager and to be admired by his staff. They were used to me back in Chicago. If they were still impressed with me, they had long stopped showing it. "You should come out to California Sol," the manager said between his lavish praises. "You'd do well out here." His flattery fueled me through most of the afternoon and while Carol and I killed some time before heading back to the airport, I casually said, "Let's go look for a house." I was only half serious, but a couple of hours and a $1,000 down payment later, we owned a home in Southern California, and I still worked in Chicago.

Driven

Leaving Chicago wasn't as easy as just deciding to go. I found that out when I called my manager Monday morning. He was furious. It might not have mattered if I was performing poorly. They probably would have helped me pack my bags. Since that was far from the case, I was told that I didn't have the option to move without the consent of the regional vice president. That man was on the phone within the hour to let me know that it was not forthcoming.

For the next 14 months, I worked harder than ever in Chicago to pay my two mortgages. The effort quickly became burdensome, especially since success had yet to fill the void in me. My numbers were always up and impressive. I had achieved a lot. My home and office were crammed with trophies and plaques, but none of them was a President's Trophy, the one award which recognized that agent who was Number One. Every year I would come close for just a moment, but when the year was over, another man would hold the prize and wear the specially-tailored red blazer that came along with it. Number One was the only award I didn't have, so I wanted it to the exclusion of everything else. Anything short of it was failure to me.

I was all drive and no joy. My relationship with my boss in Chicago was tense at best. He felt betrayed and disrespected. I felt trapped and disrespected. Neither of us was offering up any ground. Fed up, I wrote a letter to the vice president asking again to be allowed to move to California. He responded with a call to dress me down about protocol, regard for organizational structure and the hierarchy within it. Finally he said they would send me to Southern Cal, but not to work with the manager who had asked for me. Instead I went to Pasadena, to an office that was struggling under a manager I did not know. It was Thursday. They were expecting me at the new office on Monday. I left for California and Carol stayed behind to pack up our life in Chicago.

My wife and I had never bought a new house. We were so naïve we thought the money we were paying toward our mortgage was for the place we walked through over a year ago, the one with all the great furniture and the lush front yard. We didn't know that those were just models, and that our house was an empty, unadorned thing waiting for us to arrive and turn it into a home.

I spent my first night in the new house by myself shocked. There was no electricity, gas, or water. The floor was hard under my newly purchased sleeping bag. I waited to fall asleep. For a long time, I just looked around the dark room, and then fear took over as realization began to terrorize me.

What was I doing, and what was I walking my family into? Was Chicago really so horrible? I had left a place where I was established, competitive, and held in high regard by some. We had friends and family there and roots in the community. No, it wasn't comfortable, far from it, but hindsight was telling me surely it was sufferable. Nobody likes being in the frying pan at first. It's only when your feet touch the fire that it starts to look good to you. After that, every skillet experience is endured with patience and even a measure of gratitude, but my gratitude was a little late coming. My feet were already in the flames. I wouldn't learn until much later that frying pan or fire, heat is there to teach us something new about our strength, our power, the actual depth of our joy, the effectiveness of prayers, faith, integrity, and vision. All I knew that long, lonely weekend was that I was very afraid.

On Monday, I went into my new manager's office and introduced myself. After that, all I could tell him was the only thing in my head at the time. "I'm scared." I couldn't believe that was all I could tell him about myself, but it was the truth, and it was all I had. I expected him to be surprised or disappointed. Here his office is failing and the boys at the top send down a guy whose opening line is, "I'm scared"? He seemed unperturbed. He just looked at me and said, "You're a pro. You're gonna make it." It wasn't much, but it was enough. I don't know if it was his tone, or my own distress, but what I heard in subtext was, "Get up and stop feeling sorry for yourself. This is your first day on the job...*so go do your job!*"

I walked out of his office just as the phone was ringing at reception. It was the department head of a local college. Their school of theology was closing and the people there would be losing their jobs. They had called the office a few times asking if someone would come over to look at the insurance policies they had with our company and show them how to convert them. This wasn't new business, so there would be no commissions. It wasn't worth the drive out to the campus and everyone knew it, so no one would take the call."

Go do your job!

"I'll take it," I said. What else did I have to do that day except my job? I got directions to the college and headed over. Right away, it felt good to focus my attention on someone else's needs for the moment.

I was more thorough than usual with the group, explaining everything to them in great detail, answering each question, some more than a few times. Then I let my natural curiosity take over and before long I forgot about my own troubles and found myself enjoying this upbeat collection of transitioning men and women. We had a lot in common, but they weren't afraid of tomorrow. I claimed a measure of their courage as my own and despite the hours already behind me, I knew I had not wasted my time.

I'm not entirely clear on the specific path of our conversations, or the point in time when it happened, but I discovered somewhere in the mix of stories, queries, and wonderings about the future, that every person in the office was actually insurable and would be better off in the long run getting new policies instead of trying to hold onto the ones they had. I told them so and they all agreed. Spurred by that new business from the college, I ended my first week of work at the new office with an astounding 40 sales!

I took it as confirmation that leaving Chicago wasn't a mistake after all and that I was exactly where I was supposed to be. Carol and the girls soon followed and we settled into our new home. All of us adapted to life in

Southern California pretty quickly, mostly because none of us missed those Illinois winters.

It didn't take long to get back into my old groove…in every way. I worked hard and then promptly shifted to working too hard. The emptiness I woke up with every morning dogged me throughout the day and often withheld my sleep from me. I was excelling professionally, my wife was wonderful, the kids were healthy and loving their new environment, and still I had no peace. Attaining Number One or being too exhausted to care seemed to be the only options for relief…until a life-altering chain of events revealed another.

The first one caught me totally off guard. I was home alone watching television or more accurately letting it watch me. Carol and the girls were out running errands. I was flipping through channels, not settling anywhere long enough to see more than one image or hear more than a word or two. *Click. Click. Click.* My thumb and the remote were going to town.

Then I reached the station airing the program of a local minister, Pastor Jerry Bernard, and my thumb decided unexpectedly to abandon its game with the remote. "Are you looking for a church home?" he asked. It was a harmless question, but the pastor was looking directly into the camera at me. No doubt there were others being looked at the same way at that moment, but they weren't next to me on the couch. I was the one being challenged. His pointing finger was piercing me all the way to the soul. He wasn't really scolding or threatening like some pastors do, but his intensity glued my no longer wandering attention to everything he said and how he saying it.

Sometime during our "exchange" I became aware that the familiar feelings of emptiness had come to the surface in me. Normally they would drive me to busyness. This was one of those rare times that I let myself feel them in front of this man who looked like he had already found what I couldn't. He didn't offer any answers that afternoon, but he said enough to give me hope. When Carol and the girls got home, I announced that we'd be going to church Sunday.

The church was not the traditional Baptist one I was used to. It was Charismatic, lively and expressive. The congregants weren't civilly clapping like "devout people." They were raising hands, praying aloud, and singing like God was up in the rafters cupping His ear. There was emotion and intensity here. It was messy worship. The presence of God was politely entreated in the churches I grew up in. Here, they kicked down the door and hollered, "Hey, God! We're here! Let's dance!"

We started attending Pastor Bernard's church regularly. It took some getting used to, but Carol was thrilled that I wanted to go anywhere at all. I don't know what I was expecting, but it didn't take long to realize I had not found it. I watched my wife and daughters caught up in the energy of the service. They were as free as everyone else around me. I envied them. I was struggling to find a way to connect, but the loneliness of being a just spectator to their joy was all I found. I felt tormented, like I was being punished Sunday after Sunday. Finally, wondering if I should give up trying filled me with such despair that I began to pray—for the first time in a very long time—that God would change me.

I got a call a few weeks later from Pastor Bernard. He wanted to meet me for lunch. I had no idea what he wanted. Could he tell that I was only attending his church because my family loved it? Did he and God want to kick me out because they knew that I was just going through the motions?

He asked me to help him with a life insurance policy and some financial planning. How did he find me and why did he think I was the one to help him? He read my thoughts. There were others in our church who were qualified to do what he needed done, he explained, but the Holy Spirit had pointed me out specifically and he wanted to be obedient.

I reluctantly agreed to work with him. Having been down this road before, I did my job and kept my distance. He was very happy, and often felt the need to tell me that I was made for the work I was doing. He introduced me to his friends, many of whom were pastors like him. They challenged me with their specific needs and I had to educate myself to creatively provide for them.

I quickly became an "expert" in financial planning for ministries. However, while I appreciated the new business, I wouldn't give myself to it completely, and I really didn't have to. I had already built a substantial secular practice. The ministries were icing. I made sure they were never the cake.

Detour

Sharp turns on the highway are marked by a sign in the shape of a large yellow diamond with a 90° black arrow in the center of it. When your life takes a similar change in direction, it's usually unannounced.

Two car accidents in the space of six months almost ended my career in the insurance business. I injured my back in the first one and couldn't work for four weeks. Then shortly after returning to work, a second accident sent me back home for an additional four months.

Prudential was going through some transitions of its own at the time. It wanted to be viewed as more than a company that sold life insurance. The emphasis was shifting to money management and a new type of agent was being courted. They were young, aggressive, college educated men and women, savvy about investment portfolios and annuity business. They were being recruited from universities and MBA programs. In addition to that, successful investment specialists from other firms were wooed to Prudential with attractive incentives and visible, substantial executive support. They became the rock stars of the company. Agents like me who specialized in life insurance were considered the dinosaurs of the company. We weren't exactly being "phased out" but no one was fighting our extinction either.

It happened at the worst possible time. I was struggling when I returned to work. I don't know think there is anyone in sales who hasn't hit a slump. As slumps go though, this one was colossal. I couldn't sell myself to my own mother. It seemed the more I worked at it, the less I produced.

It was assumed that the business had passed by "old timers" like me. One of the vice presidents even suggested that I leave and finish out my career hawking burial policies. Just that fast, everything that made sense to me didn't anymore. The voices in the executive office became the voices in my head. "Times have changed, Sol. How do you expect to compete, with no college, primarily selling life insurance policies? You can forget Number One."

My confidence was in the basement. The only thing that got me through the day was remembering how Carol would encourage me. I'd tell her what they were saying at the office, and she wouldn't blink. "They don't know you," she'd say. "Look at all you've done, all the places you've gone." I didn't know how she could be so sure of such a broken man. It didn't occur to her to be afraid that her wellbeing—and that of our children—was in my fragile care.

Nothing changed at work. In fact it got worse. I got worse. The voices grew louder and told me over and over again that I was nothing, an uneducated failure. The emptiness I felt before was now a chasm in my soul, and in my desperation to fill it, I occupied myself wherever I felt productive. Whenever the doors of the church opened, I was there, teaching bible study, cooking, serving, and volunteering in men's ministry.

After awhile, however, the busyness got its own voice. Every time I tried to distract and pacify myself with activity, I was reminded that I was a hypocrite and a fake. I taught men about confidence and integrity but I wasn't living it. I was smiling and serving like I could afford to be generous with my attention. The truth is I was allowing people to believe they were getting me, when they were really getting a stranger playing a part.

I tried to explain that to Pastor Bernard the afternoon that I went to see him about resigning my ministry positions. I told him everything I was feeling and how lying about it had taken a huge toll on me. Carol was there hearing most of what I was saying for the first time. I think she already knew it though. She was glad I could finally unburden myself. My relief didn't last long.

The more I talked, the more vulnerable I seemed to myself. There was a heap of wreckage inside me and talking about it made it real. I felt exposed and ashamed. Quitting was necessary now, because I needed to hide. Dying inside is one thing. Turning that ugliness inside out lays your weakness before others and leaves you without your last defense, false bravado.

I don't know how long I talked. When it was over, I was shattered, miserable, and exhausted. I just wanted the pastor to release me from any further obligations to him or anyone else so I could withdraw completely.

"What did God tell you about this, Sol?" I wouldn't look at him and he knew I didn't have an answer. "I won't accept your resignation, Sol. I won't let you quit, not until you pray about it. Carol, what do you think?"

She had never seen me this low. It's one thing to talk about piety and prayer, but we all knew that religion is nothing if not practical. Faith needed to be walked out, day by day, moment by moment. All the hand raising and singing in the world means nothing if you're too destroyed on the inside to care what any of it means. I knew Carol was worried about me and I was sorry she had to defend me now, but I was too weak to defend myself. I waited for her to tell him to give me some grace. And when I saw her struggling to choose her words, I almost felt sorry for what was about to happen to the man sitting in front of us.

"I think he's right, honey." It was all she said as she looked directly at me.

"Go pray, Sol, and then come back."

I almost didn't hear him. I was still processing what Carol had just said. I barely heard her as she thanked the pastor, didn't notice that we were walking outside and paid little attention as I started the car and got on the road.

She had left me utterly alone back there. She saw me clinging to her and she let go of me. I said nothing on the ride home. I pulled the car into the driveway and turned it off. As I reached for the door handle, Carol's voice cut into the silence.

"I'm proud you didn't lie. I think your answer is

somewhere in prayer. I think you have to talk to God."

When I was sure she was finished talking, I got out of the car, without acknowledging her advice, and entered the house. I went into the guestroom, got in the bed and stared up at the ceiling. I didn't come out for dinner or play with the girls, and later, when it was time for bed, I slept there.

I had never before chosen to sleep apart from Carol. Many years later, I think about how painful that must've been for her, but I wasn't thinking that night. To her credit, she didn't challenge me or force me to do the right thing and consider her. I guess she knew I couldn't have borne that.

The next morning, the heaviness in my soul was so great I only knew that I needed to get away somewhere by myself. I was falling apart, and I couldn't pretend anymore. I didn't wake up with a plan. I was just going to drive until I stopped. I grabbed the keys and left.

Carol ran out after me carrying a bible. "I don't need that." I waved her off. She kept coming toward me. When she reached me, she held it out to me and said, "Honey please." I had no intention of using it, but I took it to avoid an argument, tossing it on the seat as I drove away.

There's a restaurant I had been to once on the beach in La Jolla. It was near a cove, and I remembered looking out at the rocks one day and noticing a cave. That's where I decided to go.

Some driving, a little beach walking, and a bit of climbing brought me to the cave. I went inside. It was dark and moist, pretty much what you'd expect. I couldn't see the ocean from where I was, so I moved closer to the opening and sat down. The bible sat beside me. I wanted to be able to tell Carol I took it with me.

For a long time, I just stared out at the water. I watched

it move in and out, up and down. The waves swelled and then flattened into ripples, their rhythm only disturbed for split seconds at a time when birds pierced the surface to retrieve their lunch.

When you don't know what you're waiting for, you're seldom ready when it arrives. The noise was quiet at first, like a distant gull. Then it got louder, lower, and uglier-sounding. By the time I realized it was coming from me, it was horrific. I was crying; bawling at first and then screaming.

Everything came out like a flood, all my anger, fear, despair, confusion, and loneliness. What had I done that God would need to punish me like this? Did He even love me? I ranted until there was nothing left. I wept like my eyes were made of water, for every disappointment I had ever hidden, for every inner voice that had tormented me.

I worked hard and had little to show for it. I was on low sales probation now and very close to being fired. Mostly, I cried because I was lost. How had I come to this place?

"Open up the Bible. I want to talk to you."

It was a "voice" so strong inside me that it was almost audible. The words were clear and there was no mistaking The Source. Shocked, then humbled and embarrassed by my rage, I picked up the book.

I read something once about our "vocation" in life being to place our ear to the chest of God and listen to His heartbeat, then with our lives, repeat to the world what we heard. For a long time I had been avoiding that kind of contact. Now here I was with no other choice, and for the first time in a long time, I didn't want another choice.

"God, I believe you're God all by yourself." I can't say it felt good to pray there in that cave, but it felt right and real for a change, so I continued. "I believe you talk to your people through your Word. By faith I'm going to open these pages. Please speak to me."

We stayed in that cave for hours. I read and listened. He comforted. I was running away. He was calling me home. He had heard my prayers. He even heard when I stopped praying. He heard my cries, and caught every fallen tear.

"You've been seeking acceptance, and I've already accepted you." I didn't have to guess what He meant. I wanted to be seen as special by everyone and in all circumstances. Being Number One was important to me because I had to prove I was the best. I didn't want people to look at me and see "less." I wanted them to see someone extraordinary. I liked beating the odds and confounding people's expectations.

"What gives you the most joy?"

The question appeared in me unexpected. I thought about Rev. Brunson and how excited I was when I first started going to that church. I thought about how badly I wanted to connect at Pastor Bernard's church. I loved serving and teaching. The answer was obvious, and that lead me to another realization. I don't know if I thought it, or if He thought it for me:

"My people are being destroyed for a lack of knowledge."

He had called me to help people by helping leaders in the church. He had called me to what gave me the most joy, but I had left it because I was disappointed that people had not accepted me.

A pattern of emotional behavior began to make itself visible. How many times had I allowed what others thought of me to drive me in one direction or another? Even when the result was positive, I saw that there was something in me that was always hungry for approval, something I already had.

I saw the source of the void in me and I understood

why failure made me so uneasy. I thought it defined me in some way, but I was learning in that cave that I was designed to walk a path that was set before me as I was being knitted together in my mother's womb. I understood for the first time, how truly unshakable the call of God is. I also understood that I was designed to enjoy that call, that anything less would not satisfy me.

I left my emptiness in that cave and went home to my wife a new man. I was a man who knew I was valued; that God had invested Himself in me, so there was nothing I had to prove but that He was God. I had put my ear to His chest and heard great and wonderful things, but also intimate and tender things as well. I was complete, and I could give to others out of that completeness, generously, without fear.

I can't begin to tell you how my newfound wisdom transformed every relationship and perspective I had. Perhaps that's another book for another time. I will say here that, after that day, I asked for and gave much grace to the people I cared for and worked with. I saw my own heart and daily I began to ask God to clean it out. I gave myself to helping leaders, particularly in ministry, plan for their financial futures. I gave myself with joy. Mostly, I prayed. I asked for answers. I cherished my peace.

I didn't expect anything when I left the house that morning. God gave me what I couldn't ask for, couldn't do for myself, and couldn't live without. I returned with a miracle.

Inner Space

I want real success. I want success that gives me confidence, fulfillment, and joy. My confidence comes from knowing that I am valuable to God, even when the world can't see it. I am fulfilled because He has invested Himself in me, and I am complete, even while I'm still moving toward my goals. Finally, if I believe what He says about me, when I put my ear to His chest, I will have joy, even in dark places. I want to live my life secure, generously, and without fear. God, tell me what's in your heart about me.

Read this prayer a few times. Write about any thoughts or feelings that prevent you from praying it for yourself? If there are none, re-write the prayer as your own, expanding on each part of it as thoughts come to you. Take your time. Write until the thoughts stop coming.

Think and write about 1 person who counts on you, 2 things you're afraid of, and 3 people or causes you would invest yourself in if you had the time and resources.

God,

I want to be successful, I want to enjoy everything that life has to offer as it pertains to fruitful living. But I don't want to be successful at the cost of losing my relationship with you. Lord, I desire to always live Holy & upright, I never want to bring shame to your name. Keep me pure & Holy. Keep me even when I don't want to be kept. I want to be a great provider for my family. I want to be able to walk confidently & to be able articulate words correctly & speak clear & consise. God, I need you. I know that it's by your power & might that I am able to fulfill your will in the earth. Show me God, who I really am in you. Show me how you really see me. Blow my mind & reveal unto me the things that you are just waiting to manifest in my life. God allow me to see the REAL ME. Take me back to before the foundation of the world & let me know the things that are necessary for my survival in this earth. Show me Lord, Show me.....

① Josh ② Failing & messing up ③ Building up young men, Rebuilding the City of B'ham + Tusc., & pushing forth the vision of Bishop L. Spenser Smith.

CHAPTER EIGHT

Let It Shine

The blessing of the Lord brings wealth, and he adds no trouble to it.

—SOLOMON (PROVERBS 10:22)

In the right light, at the right time, everything is extraordinary.

— AARON ROSE

Greatness always begins with a good long look in the mirror, and even requires a periodic revisit, but it never ever ends there.

—SOL HICKS

ॐ ॐ

"*Father...thank you...for letting me fly this flight...for the privilege of being able to be in this position, to be in this wondrous place, seeing all these many startling, wonderful things that you have created.*"

Astronaut L. Gordon Cooper, Jr. found these words in him as he became one of the first men to view the earth from space. This could be my prayer. They are certainly my thoughts, even if I'm not the first to utter them aloud.

Like Cooper, I believe I'm seeing what has never been seen before, and becoming a man no one has ever known.

When basketball phenomenon Michael Jordan entered college, everyone assumed he would do great things. He had already proven many times over that he was not afraid of grand accomplishments or the work that produces them. He saw the basket and the path to it with different eyes, and could move his body as quickly as he thought about moving it. When you watched him play he would treat you to blinding glimpses of what was to come. Even if you were a casual fan of the sport—something inside you whispered, "This kid could change the game forever."

How do you handle history-making potential? How do you see God-sized treasure in a common, often fractured human vessel? How do you steward greatness? These are not questions for a special few. I'm asking every person whose eyes are falling upon this page. Every parent should ask them the moment mommy's belly starts to swell. Teachers should ask them on the first day of school about every student instead of waiting for the last day to see which ones get the A's. I ask every "ordinary" man or woman I encounter. It doesn't occur to most of us that these questions follow all of us into the world.

Every answer was waiting for Michael Jordan when he arrived at the University of North Carolina and met Coach Dean Smith who told him, "Michael, if you can't pass, you can't play." Translation: Greatness begins with a good long look in the mirror, and even requires a periodic revisit, but it never ever ends there. Individuals score. Teams win.

Eyes on the Real Prize

I thought I knew what I wanted before I entered that cave in LaJolla. When I left it, a different understanding was fueling my drive. There is purpose attached to each of us, and people will be attracted to us because of it. Our purpose is to use our time, talent, and treasure to improve the lives of those people. Our families should be more secure because of us. Clients should be better off after we have worked with them. We do what we do for bigger reasons than a paycheck, or a trophy, and then those things become a by-product of our efforts.

At the end of the day—and at the beginning if we're honest—our success in the world is related to and solidified by our value to the people we encounter and impact in the world. It's not their permission or acceptance we need. That would be a measure of their value to us. It's the "you-shaped holes" in their lives that reveal your path, and your willingness to serve that guarantees irrevocable rewards.

My focus after my cave experience shifted from myself to others. The truth is I was more comfortable in that mode, but I thought that winning meant keeping personal distractions to a minimum. In my mind I was an athlete always after the score. If I turned my head to the right or the left it would only slow me down. My eyes, I determined, should stay on "the prize." The shift happened when I learned that my joy and my success didn't have to contend with one another. If I saw the prize as the people I loved, worked with, and served, the win was always in my grasp, because they would see to it. It was not just my success but *ours* that would be at stake.

As an adolescent, Michael Jordan could see his way to the basket from anywhere on the court. In college he learned to see his team, and by passing away the ball he was so deft at handling, and letting others score, he taught them to see the game as he saw it, love it as he did, and want to win as badly as he did. By the time he made it to the Chicago

Bulls, Michael had become "Air," a powerful, unstoppable, often invisible force moving, pushing, leading best from behind, flinging obstacles to the wayside or eroding them over time, and lifting everything in its course. Carried by a strong wind, everyone believes they can fly.

So it is with us. We were put here to make history, not merely repeat it, thereby letting it make us. Like L. Gordon Cooper and Air Jordan, we were made to fly, and also like them, not by ourselves. By allowing others to become a part of our desires, and by becoming a part of theirs, winning is more often a conclusion than a question because we're all invested in it. Embracing that perspective changed my life.

U.S. Supreme Court Justice Thurgood Marshall said, "None of us has gotten where we are solely by pulling ourselves up from our own bootstraps. We got here because somebody bent down and helped us." My wife and Pastor Bernard helped me when I was down. My children inspired me. My clients and friends continually encouraged and supported me. Even difficult relationships blessed me in their own refining way. I had a lot to be grateful for and I decided to spend my days giving back to those who had given so much to me.

I had never known so much fulfillment. I was truly free for the first time in my life. I lacked nothing and every experience tasted heavenly. At work, I became curious again, and then intensely interested in people; not in what they could add or take away from me, but in *them*. I set about repairing broken relationships. In that failing season at work I had allowed my anger and frustration to plant some bitterness in my heart. Asking for forgiveness from those I thought had injured me released me to succeed either with them or in spite of them. The choice was theirs.

I began speaking at company workshops again. I also

became a mentor to new agents. They became the focus of most of my energy, and teaching them only sharpened my own skills. My numbers were way up. I noticed it, but it wasn't driving me now. I was glad for the opportunity to share what I knew, to help other agents overcome whatever obstacles were facing them and help them avoid some of the ones that caused me to falter. Number One would be nice, but not at the expense of giving back.

Then one day, following my presentation at a company workshop, Carol came up and whispered in my ear. "You're going to be Number One," she told me. I had learned two things about my bride very early in our relationship. First, she's a woman of few words. She's not coy, and she doesn't flatter you unnecessarily. She is one of the most sincere communicators I know. Second, she's usually right. A wise counselor is a wonderful gift, and I treasure the one I have in my wife. "When, baby?" was all I asked her.

"This year."

I took a good look at her. Her expression wasn't one I hadn't seen before. Sometimes Carol can say, without words, "I know what I said, and I didn't stutter. Now if you want me to repeat it, I will, but you're not going to hear anything different."

Let me put this in perspective for you. There were 12 qualifying days left in the year. We were currently 135th in line for Number One. I was sure that more fantastic things had happened in history, though I couldn't think of a single one at that moment. Still, I knew the God who had restored me and given me back my joy was capable of anything. I knew that "impossible" was only in His dictionary to describe life without Him.

We approached my manager and asked for some blank applications. He wanted to know how many, and wanting to show my wife that I was on board with her, I confidently asked for 45. That was a lot of apps, and my manager said as much. I was about to explain that I was planning to be really aggressive in my last couple of weeks, but Carol spoke up.

"Give him 90."

I have to congratulate myself here for keeping my composure when my manager's brows when up and his jaw dropped. More impressive though was Carol. She didn't elaborate on her outrageous request or make any promises. She didn't try to bolster the disbelieving manager's confidence or try to charm him into catching the vision with us. She just gave him the same look she had given me only moments ago. *I know what I said, and I didn't stutter. Now, if you want me to repeat it, I will, but you're not going to hear anything different.*

My manager was a smart man. He gave us the apps, and I suspect he was saving his "I told you so" for later. He never got to use it. In 12 days, we wrote business on those 90 apps and then some. By 5:00 pm on the last qualifying day, we were Number One.

That first place trophy was sweeter than I had imagined it would be, because I never took my eyes off of the people on the path with me, my clients, friends, family, and the people I worked with. Knowing them was the prize on the way to the prize. I knew what their dreams were and how I fit into them. I shared my own dream and made them a part of it. We served one another, and when I won, I didn't enjoy it alone. They were with me.

Malcolm Forbes said, "When you cease to dream, you cease to live." I would modify that to say that when you dream alone, you cease to live. I would win six more President's Trophies, for a total of seven, in just ten short years. No one had ever accomplished such a feat, but I'm not naïve. It would not have happened in my own imagination, much less in practice, had my dreams not been joined in flight to the dreams of others. This wonderful life I've received was found in what I have been able to give.

Page Turners

I don't have a lot of time to read for leisure these days, except when I'm on vacation. When I do, I try hard to resist a nagging habit which goes back some years. I used to get a book and read a chapter or two in. If I came across a particularly tragic character, I would find it hard to read too much more before skipping to the end of the book to see if everything worked out for them. If it didn't, I wouldn't finish the book. I'd just start a new one.

It would be nice if life were like that, wouldn't it? If we knew that all would be well for us in the end, trials would be easier to endure I think. More to the point, if we could skip to the end, we could cut out the trial altogether.

But life isn't like that. We're not given the option of knowing how it will end or when that end will come. We don't know how long we have to endure difficult or dark seasons. And we can't know the consequences of our choices, good or bad, ahead of an appointed time. Like a boxer, we have to live our life round to round, moment to moment, until the end of it, certain of only one thing: If we quit, we will surely lose.

If science and history are to be believed, my life is more than half over. A birthday looms as I pen the last chapters of this work. My thoughts naturally turn to the part of my journey that is behind me, and as I attempt to sum up more than six decades of living, Oprah Winfrey's *O Magazine* enters my mind. The talk show maven writes a regular column simply titled "What I Know For Sure." I thought that would be a good place to start as I consider what I would leave you with.

I know that my wife is the single greatest gift I've ever received next to my salvation in Christ. I know that my daughters are good women and that their children, my four grandbabies, have much to offer the world. I know that my sisters are generous and that our mother is a fierce and determined beauty. I know that my life would not be what it is without them and others too numerous to mention justly. Beyond that, I don't want to burden you with what I know for sure, because truthfully, all I really know is how to live *my* life, and I'd hate to see you waste your time trying to doing that.

With all due respect to the amazing Ms. Winfrey, what I know for sure is that you are uniquely relevant to the world. You have a light that belongs to you and you alone. Finding it is your life's work. Allowing it to shine in service to others is your purpose. If you're willing, you will become a star like no other, doing what's never been done, touching lives that only you can touch, shaping, influencing, and inspiring others to do the same. You will know for sure what only you can know.

You were fashioned for a better life than the ones you've already seen, no matter how spectacular they look to you. Your life is in you waiting to be discovered by you. If I didn't believe that, I'd be little more than an angry, southern boy trapped in a man's body. The world I grew up in would never have imagined this life for me. As much as my mother, Miss Solita, Dr. McCoo, Mr. Levine, and so many others loved me, they could not desire it for me. My lovely and wise wife could not choose it for me even if she did believe it was possible.

Living your unique and extraordinary life is no small thing. It's even a little frightening. But please don't let that stop you. If you wait to be unafraid before you step onto your path, you'll never do it. It's impossible to move without fear until you have learned to move with it. The decision to make yourself more powerful than you are takes faith. Faith takes courage, and there is no courage without fear to overcome.

Resisting the urge to skip to the end of a book isn't easy, but I manage to do it now more often than not. When I do, I find that I enjoy the story so much more. Likewise, when we live out each day of our lives, moment by moment, season by season, inhabiting each morsel with the measures of strength, peace, longsuffering, and gratitude given to us, our joy becomes complete.

That I know for sure.

Obey Your Thirst

White Only.

I end my story here, at this sign. There were many of them around town, some on public bathrooms, others on drinking fountains. Most Eufaulians, black and white alike, didn't take much notice of them. They were "normal," like a stop sign, the price of gas, or the name of the bank.

There was one fountain at the drive-thru diner where I worked. I passed by it every day and touched it only to clean it, but the sign above it clearly communicated that I was never to drink from it. I wondered sometimes what "white water" tasted like. I knew better than to ask, though I wanted to badly.

As time went on, that fountain began to tempt me, like some forbidden porcelain tree in the center of the fast-food garden I lived in. The more I thought about it, the more

I wanted to taste the water I couldn't have, until finally I made up my mind to do it. I waited until everyone had gone home, then checking to make sure no one was driving by, I walked over to the fountain, frightened but determined, and took a quick sloppy slurp of the white water. I swallowed it in one gulp. It felt and tasted like…*water?*

I expected white water to be different, *holier* even; in some way better than the water I was allowed to drink. I was disappointed. It wasn't sacred at all. It was just separate. The knowledge settled into me, roughly at first, and then a thought occurred to me.

If the water inside that fountain was no different than the water inside the ones I drank from, then maybe the people who drank from it weren't so different on the inside from me. I didn't know if that was true or not, but the possibility was comforting.

As I end this chapter, I am struck by how much that one act of little boy courage has shaped my thinking. Success, it seems to me, is like that "White Only" drinking fountain. People will pass by it or look at it from afar, and assume it's not for them. They will long for it, then look at the past, their failures, their lack or the limitations of their circumstances, and convince themselves that success is a different life, meant for different people, better people. Don't believe it. Success is your legacy as long as you decide to reach for it.

Expect to be told that you are not entitled to live an astonishing existence. Then remember that you are God's plan A and there is no plan B, and then make up your mind to do it anyway. I promise you, nothing will be more satisfying or useful to the world than the brilliant, powerful, extraordinary revelation of the story of YOU.

Inner Space

We succeed not at the end of our lives, but throughout our lives, moment by moment, grace to grace, faith to faith. Success is not waiting for me to reach it someday. Rather it's expecting me to reach for it everyday. Daily, I want to become more fully "me." I want to know what only I can know, and help others find the courage to do the same.

Read this paragraph a few times. What thoughts, people, or feelings come up as you reflect on the challenges in it?

Think and write about **1** thing that's priceless to you, **2** God-sized dreams, and **3** ways you're already succeeding.

1) My relationship w/ God is priceless to me.!!

2) God sized dreams are Opulence Magazine + Turning Probe, LLC marketing + Graphic Design in to an enterprise for multiple businesses.

3) I'm already succeeding in keeping my marriage healthy & happy; Stepping out to move in the direction of entrepreneurship; succeeding in keeping my relationship w/ God healthy.

God, I want to make an Impact in the world

Not just because I want my name to be called but because there are so many people who desire help. I understand God that you have called me out & set me apart, so that I may be able to help you transform people's lives & straighten their mindset out to believing in the impossible. God of course I want to leave a legacy, but I ultimately want my life to matter to someone who desires an intimate encounter w/ you, but the only tangible resource they may have is me. (in this earth realm). God, allow me to do my part. Don't let me leave this earth with my work undone. Reveal unto me those things that I am suppose to be doing now for this season of my life.

CHAPTER ~~NINE~~ MINE

Now It's Personal

The quiet words of the wise are more to be heeded than the shouts of a ruler of fools.

—SOLOMON (ECCLESIASTES 9:17)

Life loves to be taken by the lapel and told: "I'm with you kid. Let's go."

— MAYA ANGELOU

My life matters. It's worth living moment by moment, season to season. Success simply confirms that fact.

—YOUR NAME HERE

❧ ❦

We've come to the end of my stories. I hope that means you've begun to uncover some of your own. As you look over what you've written throughout this book, what are the stories from your own life which come to mind? Jot down one- or two-word titles for each one. They can be pleasant stories, or painful ones, recent or from long ago. If it is an event that impacted, transformed, or interrupted your journey, it's worthy of mention. All your stories are significant, because they contributed to shaping who you are.

Don't over think. Don't edit yourself. If it comes up in you, don't spend any time reasoning about it yet. Just write it down in a phrase that will help you remember it later. If you need more space, take it. That's a good thing.

1. _____

2. _____

3. _____

4. _____

5. _____

6. _____

7. _____

8. _____

9. _____

"I never did anything worth doing by accident, nor did any of my inventions come by accident; they came by work." When Plato said that, I don't know if he was thinking about the work that goes into examining a life. Hopefully he was, because I think that's the most worthwhile work any of us can do, especially if our success in life is in any way connected to serving or influencing others. That said, it's time to get a good look at you.

Read over what you wrote down in Chapter One. Now

that you've had a little more time to think about it, are there things you want to add, remove, or change? What stands out to you in what you've written? Do you have more clarity about anything than you did when you started this book? Are there desires which surfaced that you weren't aware you had? In the space below, be more specific about who you are, what you want, and how you impact your environment.

_____

_____

_____

_____

_____

_____

_____

_____

_____

_____

_____

_____

A Second Opinion
EXERCISE #1

In the table below, write three words that describe 1) how you see yourself, 2) how you think others see you, and 3) your approach to problem-solving.

How I See Myself	How Others See Me	Problem-Solving Approach

Now find one or two people whose thinking you respect. Choose someone who knows you well enough to have some opinions about you and is willing to share them. You should trust that they will be truthful, even if they have something hard to say to you. If you're not sure, verbally give them permission to be that way, but if you're sensitive, it's all right to ask them to be gentle with their communication. Keep in mind that if you are sensitive, you might be better off choosing only one person to keep from feeling "ganged up on" if they have something negative to say. It's easy to withdraw or get defensive if that happens.

Ask them the same questions about you and write their responses in the table with your own. Take some time to discuss all of your thoughts. Afterwards, consider how you felt during your time of sharing. Did you find what the person(s) had to say valid, or were they "off base" in your opinion? Did you feel heard and seen, or just exposed and vulnerable? Do you get the sense that they're thinking independently, or just telling you what you want to hear? If you are satisfied that you are safe with your person(s), continue through the rest of the exercises. If not, choose someone else and begin again with the first one.

EXERCISE #2

Talk to your friend about what you've written at the end of the chapters of this book. Ask them to listen as you tell them about yourself, your dreams, your fears, and your thoughts. Invite them to interrupt you and ask for clarity at any point, but not to weigh in with an opinion just yet. If you're really feeling courageous, hand your book over to them and let them read it.

When you're finished, have three (3) discussions: first, talk about **what you said** that impacted the person and why. Second, talk about **what you didn't say**. What was left out? What questions came up for your listener as you talked to him/her? Is there something you're avoiding or in denial about that they can point out to you? Is there something you said that they weren't really convinced about? Are there issues "underneath" what you said that are worth exploring? For example, is there some bitterness, envy, vengeance, or disappointment that should at least be acknowledged, even if it isn't discussed at length? Be careful with this conversation. Communication on both sides should be kind, honest, and other-centered. In other words, the person you're talking to is always more important than what you have to say, and how they actually receive your words is more important than your intention when you said them.

Lastly, you should talk about **what you're fashioned to say**. This can be an enlightening and fun time of discovery if you give yourself over to it. After hearing what you had to say about yourself, ask your friend to think about what things you are best equipped to say to others. What special knowledge and understanding has been put into you by your life's experiences? What themes repeat themselves in your life? What lessons are you best at teaching? How can you encourage others? What have you overcome that you can model for others? How have you and do you inspire and influence the people you connect with? What's great about you? What makes you "special," in general and specifically to the eyes and heart of that person?

As they talk to you, write down what impacts you, what they say that you didn't know, and how you feel in the space below. Were there any surprises for you?

_____

_____

_____

_____

_____

_____

_____

_____

_____

_____

_____

_____

_____

_____

_____

_____

EXERCISE #3

This is going to require some faith on both sides. In light of all that you have said and learned, agree on three things to pray for your life. Look through your book if you have to. You can pray about your dreams, your relationships, a goal, or an emotional issue. You can pray about a bad habit, or ask for a good one. Nothing is off limits.

There are only two restrictions: 1) You have to pray aloud so you can hear one another, and 2) you can't start praying until you both have talked about everything you're grateful for, including and especially each other. Spend some time on your past, your present, and even think about the future and what you believe can happen.

Write your prayers in the margins of these pages before you begin so you won't forget them. Pray using whatever words are most comfortable for you. There's nothing mystical about what you're doing. On the contrary, it's very practical. Two hearts to care, two sets of eyes to see, another source of light, and accountability; what could be more practical?

My Prayer For You

Lord,

I believe You are good, and that You can do anything because all power is in Your hands. As Your sons and daughters seek to navigate their way through this world, show them a well-lit path. In those seasons where they must walk through the dark, teach them how to recognize Your still, small, voice whispering in their ears. And if they ever find themselves without ears that hear or eyes that see, if they find themselves far from home, I pray that they will have put Your Word in their hearts to remind them that they matter to You even when they don't believe they matter to anyone else.

God, show them their gifts, talents, and resources, and then teach them to be kind and generous. Don't let them waste time worrying about how they will succeed. You open doors that no man can shut. You don't make anything to fail. You know everything, and there is no place we can go where You cannot meet us and love us. Success is ours because You are with us.

Honor the prayers they have written on these pages. In fact, give them more than they've asked for. Give them as much power, wisdom, and joy as they can handle. Give them as much wealth as they can steward well, and continue to increase their capacity for it. Bless their families and let them be blessed by their families. Father, do more for them, in them, and through them than they can imagine is possible.

Take their eyes off of every standard for success except the one You placed inside them. Thank You for the privilege of telling my story. Make them courageous enough to tell theirs. Remind them daily that the world needs to hear their voice, and see their light.

I love You, and I love them,
Amen.